Sᴴᴇɪᴋʜ Nᴀᴢɪᴍ ᴀʟ HᴀQQᴀɴɪ:

Pᴜʀᴇ Hᴇᴀʀᴛs

12-5-99

With Love and
prayers for a
pure Heart.

PURE
HEARTS

1997 & 1998 associations in
Great Britain, Spain & the USA
with a Sufi Master of our time

SHEIKH NAZIM
AL HAQQANI

HEALING HEARTS
ZERO PRODUCTIONS
LONDON

Published by:
Healing Hearts / Zero Productions, London
collected, edited, commented and typeset by Zero

cover: Ceiling of the Mohamed Ali Mosque in Cairo

photograph of Sheikh Nazim by Ahmed Isa Fuchs

British Library Cataloguing in Publication Data.
A catalogue record of this book is available from the British
Library.

Printed and bound by TIRA, Prague

ISBN 1-898863-19-9

Contents:

WHO IS SHEIKH NAZIM? WHAT IS HIS MISSION?

"The sun will rise in the West!" proclaimed the Prophet Muhammad*. And so, Sheikh Nazim was sent to Europe to prepare the people for these new enlightened times. All 'isms' are coming to an end. People are starting to realise that their mind-produced systems are not leading them to the happiness and peace they are looking for. The West is yearning for a spiritual sign, for some connection to a reality beyond the never-satisfying materialism.

Maulana Sheikh Nazim al Haqqani is such a connection. The wisdom he shares with us is not his own. He is transmitting from a chain of holy people. He is the 40th Sheikh in the Golden Chain of the Naqshbandia Tariqat[1], which leads back to the Prophet Muhammad* as the first recipient of Divine Knowledge within this line.

Sheikh Nazim has been coming regularly to London for the Holy Month of Ramadan since 1974. He was given this order by Sheikh Abdullah Daghistani. He was told that the Last Days had begun and truth would once more become apparent, this time coming from the West.

---

* It is a custom to show respect and to add, "May peace be upon him." after mentioning the name of a prophet. To avoid a lengthy repetition, the* will symbolise this greeting throughout the text.

---

[1] see: The Golden Chain of the Naqshbandiyya Tariqat

The extraordinary success of Sheikh Nazim in bringing Islam back to the hearts of westerners, in the midst of ever-growing official condemnation of this religion, is a clear sign of what his followers continuously experience: his Holiness. We have been told that there are 124,000 Holy People alive all the time. In our days most of them are hidden. Sheikh Nazim too, had a dream of spending the rest of his life in seclusion:

He was born on the 21.4.1922 in Larnaca, Cyprus. Although known to have been a pious child, his complete dedication to a spiritual life did not come until he was in his twenties. He was studying chemistry in Istanbul, when his brother who was suffering of TB, died in his arms. This changed his whole life. He realised how limited medicine, science and this worldly life in general is, and began his spiritual quest.

His first step was a year long seclusion in Aleppo, spent in a cellar, praying and eating only 7 olives a day. After a year the sheikh there told him he had reached such a level, that there was only one sheikh who could now help him: Sheikh Abdullah Daghistani in Damascus. Sheikh Nazim set out at once to meet this sheikh and had only one wish, to ask Sheikh Abdullah for permission to spend the rest of his life in seclusion at the tomb of Muhammad* in Medina. Instead, he was sent off to be constantly surrounded by people, to train them and to be an example for them, first in Cyprus, then in London. "It is the end of time", he was told, "and particularly people in the West need holy inspiration to illuminate their hearts and lead them out of the abyss of darkness."

WHAT ARE HOLY PEOPLE?

For most people in the West, Holy People are something of the past, people engraved in statues or captured on paintings. The presumption of holy people still being alive today in our secularised, positivistic world, almost seems out of time. Yet there are 124 000 Holy People alive all the time. So what are their particulars?

The word 'holy' comes from whole, complete. It signifies a person who has reached wholeness, who is complete in the sense that he is following the Will of the Creator in everything. Allah Almighty has regularly sent down exact recipes of how we can attain holiness, by following His Holy Rules. After all, we were created in His Image, to be His representatives, His caliphs, here on earth.

This is the good news. The Creator did not just dump us here on earth and leave us to ourselves. We were given rules and instructions of how to live in peace, by following His Rules and so fulfilling our purpose here on earth: to return to HIM.

In our days we are filled with the misconception of being free. Of course we have a will to choose between good and evil, this is what characterises us and gives us responsibility. We can choose to lead an evil life by totally ignoring the Holy Instructions our Creator has given us. We must, on the other hand, recognise that for every disobedience there is a price to pay, either now, or in the hereafter. And the price increases, the longer you wait, the more expensive it will be. Because of this, every person with any sense at all, should strive to do good. It is the mission of every Holy Person, like Sheikh Nazim, to teach us precisely that, to be good.

People following a Holy Master like Sheikh Nazim, have the advantage of seeing these Holy Laws lived and demonstrated with every move. At the same time, the Holy Energy which emanates from a Holy Person, hits everyone who comes into contact with them straight into the heart. When love has awoken, a follower cannot but magnetically follow such a master, who will lead them out of the chaos of their egotistical desires and back to the source, back to the Creator. That is their task.

Sheikh Nazim was once asked how it is possible for Holy People to sometimes be physically at several places at the same time. He described it as a procedure where, once you master every single part of your physical body with your will-power, you can dress your physical body with your spiritual body. Meaning, your spiritual body is then no longer imprisoned in your physical body, instead you pull your spiritual body over the physical. Then physical laws like time and space do not apply anymore. You can then even fly to Heaven without wings, just using your will-power.

The condition for such powers is that a person is completely in charge, that the will-power controls, not the desires. A person on such a level is holy and will not act according to their own will, but to His: Thy Will be done.

London, December 1998
Zara Zero T.Quensel

LIFE IS A BUILDING

100 years ago we were nothing and in 50 years we will be nothing. We come from nothing and we will be nothing. Within this nothingness we are trying to be something. There is a reality which makes nothing into something and then something into nothing. There must be someone who takes us from nothing to something.

That is the first message every teacher should give to his students. He should give them the name of the One Who has so many names in so many languages, a supreme neverending eternal being. Tell them, "You are now 10, 12, 15, 20... years old. 30 years ago you were nothing. Look at where you are now. You were in the wombs of your mothers, but you did not know anything. While you were growing you started to know things. Who was it who brought you from unknown to known areas?" Ask them this and teach them! That is important for the lives of everyone, especially for the new generation.

Life of man is a building. Everyone who comes into this life has been offered to build his life. That building must be strong enough to shelter people to continue safely and honourably throughout their life. It must be based on a foundation. The stronger it is, the stronger the building will be able to stand on it. If it is weak, even the wind can pull it down, or if a strong person hits on it, it will fall. It cannot be safe. This is why we need a strong foundation on which we can build a strong building of life.

Foundations are not visible, they are secret, like the roots of trees. If a tree has no roots it cannot live, like we cannot live a strong and honourable life without a foundation. Our beliefs are our strong foundation. Try to give the young people the message of Heavens which hasn't changed throughout thousands of years. It has been brought to us by Messengers and Holy Books.

This is the first information we must give young ones: we are created by the Creator of the universe. If they ask where He is, you may say, "He is beyond this universe. If you can go beyond this universe, you may see him!"

It is impossible for us to even reach the limits of this universe. Every greatness beside the greatness of the Creator will always be nothing. The universe is in limits. Beyond the universe are endless unlimited existences; darkness. He is so big that it is impossible to give a vision of Him to you. Don't think that if you bring a postcard with His image, it could represent Him. That would be foolish! His greatness is endless and unlimited. What ever He has created will be less and in limits. It will be nothing.

This is why you must say that the whole creation, all creatures need a Creator. We do not need to ask where He is and how He is. If that is what you want to know, you are asking for the impossible. It is like someone saying, "I must look at the sun and see what it is and how it is. It is impossible to enter there and to look. You would vanish. If you wanted to enter an atom and to look it would be just as impossible! We have been offered to believe. When you come to the limit of the impossible you can ask for everything which is possible. But when you ask for the limits of the impossible don't ask, because your mentality will not be able to enter. In our days atheists are the people

-12-

of satan. They create so much to cause people not to believe in anything. They invent these stupid questions to destroy beliefs. All religious people are complaining of those devils; the Jews, the Christians and the Muslims, because we all know that their aim is to destroy beliefs. Without beliefs man cannot live.

Not everything your eyes show you is true. So many times your eyes will cheat you. It will call the spot of light in the sky a spot of light, even though it is a huge galaxy with billions of stars. What is true? What your eyes see, or what your mind is telling you?

The message which you must give to children is to believe. You can find so many examples to make them believe. Give them a strong belief as a foundation. The strongest belief is to believe in the Creator. When they believe in His existence, don't worry.

We hope that youngsters now will come closer to spiritual aspects, that they will start to ask about unseen and unknown worlds. It is a grant of the Creator to them to make them believe in Him. When they believe in Him they will start asking about themselves. "Why did He create us? What is our mission? What have we been created for?" The answers to these questions will come when the building starts to evolve.

SOUL: THE ELECTRICITY OF OUR BODY

When a lady is pregnant a form of a human is created within 3 times 40 days. But it is only a piece of flesh, without any movement or any sign of life. Then suddenly its heart begins to beat and the body starts to move. There is now a new guest who has been sent to this world. It has not been sent from the material world, but from somewhere else. We cannot see it, but we know it as the spiritual world.

There are two worlds: the material and the spiritual. Finally the soul, which belongs to the spiritual world, comes into the body and the baby will develop quickly. He will prepare himself to come to this world, to be here; to grow, to know, to learn, to do, to feel and to understand. Then he must leave everything of this material world, even his body in which he has been for so many years, and go back.

No-one sees how the soul comes. No-one sees our souls leave, because they do not belong to this world. Can you see electricity? Can you cut it? It is something else. It is from the Divine Heavens. The soul is the electricity of our bodies. The power of electricity kills! The power of the soul keeps us alive!

NEVERENDING WORLDS OF ENLIGHTENMENT

If we have no connections to Heavens we will be like a cassette, only able to speak as long as there is a recording on it. When it is finished we will stop. We ask for something which is neverending. We are preparing ourselves to reach a neverending life with neverending power, knowledge, wisdom, feelings and understanding. We are running after neverending qualities. That is our pleasure.

In this world we are imprisoned, all of mankind is. We listen in limits, we hear in limits, we smell in limits, we taste in limits, we move in limits and you understand in limits, your knowledge is in limits. Everything you have been granted is in limits. If someone is in limits, they are imprisoned.

The Lord of Heavens has given everyone a chance to use these limited powers to make a connection to the neverending worlds, neverending universes and never-ending oceans. You are like a drop, when you reach the ocean you will become the ocean, you will be finished. You cannot take it back. It belongs to the ocean and will become part of it. It will be the ocean. Everyone has this chance. If you don't take it, you will always be in limits.

The ones who have reached a connection to Heavens are in the neverending spheres. The first level of Heavens, the second Heaven, the third Heaven... each level gets larger and larger and includes the previous one: the second includes the first, the third includes the second, the fourth the third, the fifth the fourth, the sixth the fifth and the seventh the sixth. That is the limit for creatures. Only prophets are allowed to move beyond. This is what happens when the drop becomes one in the endless oceans. Lucky are the ones who ask to be connected to Heavens, those who are interested. Those who don't during their lifetime must reach a connection in their last moment. It is impossible for anyone to reach the last moment without having a connection to Heavens. Some people reach the level of the First Heavens, but do not have enough to pass over to the next.

Allah the Almighty causes some people to belong and to be connected to earth, others to Heavens. Those who never reached any connection during their lives will reach the level of the First Heaven, but cannot pass through it to the next, because they belong much more to earth than to Heavens. Finally everyone must reach Heavens, but if you can reach it now, by using Heavenly Steps, you will get higher. If you do not, you are like an insect or a creature who only walks on earth, unable to get up.

People must come back to their connection. Those who are connected to Heavens will reach the enlightened worlds. The souls who are not interested in Heavens, only in this earth, will continue their travelling, development, improvement and their interest without reaching any lights. Their enjoyment will come out of darkness, out of the worlds of darkness. They will never find any enjoyment in the world of lights.

It is important in the life of man to ask for a connection to the enlightened worlds. You cannot do this without contacting someone from that world. If you ask for lights, you must ask for an enlightened person who is connected to the enlightened worlds. People who live in darkness cannot give you any lights. You will become like them: on earth, under earth or on the first, second, third, fourth, fifth, sixth or seventh level of darkness. Like the levels of light, every new level of darkness includes the previous one.

It is important in our life to find a person who belongs to Heavens. To be with him and to follow him.

This is a summary of all Heavenly Teachings. Unfortunately our physical desires usually pull us into the worlds of heaviness and darkness. Physical lights depend on those dark worlds. Without our bodies our souls could never become enlightened. People are mostly imprisoned in their physical bodies. Only a few out of hundreds, thousands, ten thousands, hundred thousands or millions of people, a very small group, is able to be interested in the enlightened world. If you are, you must reach it.

Nowadays people are usually interested in their physical desires, even though these come and go so quickly, to finish and to vanish. Spiritual enjoyment, peace and contentment, continues endlessly. Our mission is to call people out of the darkness of their physical bodies into the lights of enlightened souls in the Divine Presence. Every second their enlightenment will increase in a neverending enlightening. The neverending enjoyment continues, the neverending beauty continues, the neverending wisdom continues, neverending, neverending... They will belong to the neverending worlds. That is the honour and target of mankind, to endlessly belong to the enlightened worlds.

THE FIRST DIVINE REQUIREMENT: GOOD MANNERS

No rank is above the rank of *adab*, good manners. It is the first required attribute in the Divine Presence. No-one can enter the Divine Presence of Allah the Almighty without it. Not with gold, money, jewels, beauty, power, knowledge, ranks... It is *adab* which brings a servant closer to the Divine Presence. Divine Protocol demands those who have good manners to come first.

All Holy Books teach people good manners. Try to learn to be praised ones here and in the hereafter. It is not easy to be praised in the Divine Presence. It depends on your *adab*. Muhammad* said, "My Lord taught me good manners. He is my teacher!" We will never reach the perfection of humanity without reaching out to the traditions which he passed on to us.

People in this world are so happy when they are VIPs. They try so hard to become VIPs. It means nothing and will not give you any values. Try to be a VIP in the Divine Presence. *Adab* will make you a VIP in the Divine Presence.

Adab is something else than praying, fasting and reading the Holy Quran a lot. Tariqats teach people good manners and respect. If someone does not accept a teacher, he does not have any *adab*. The Prophet* accepted Gabriel as his teacher. He listened and obeyed him. Everyone must have a master to teach them. They accept needing one when it comes to knowledge, but not to *adab*. Knowledge is not the most important. No-one can know more than satan. Science comes completely from knowledge. Satan has such great knowledge, but he has no *adab*. He told Allah, "You did a mistake by creating Adam* and honouring him. That rank should have been mine!" This is why he was cursed and kicked out of Heaven.

Don't think that *adab* is easy. Knowledge can be learned by everyone, *adab* only by very few. Oh believers, try to reach high *adab*. It will make you much more acceptable in the Divine Presence. It will put your ego down and mercy and blessings will rain on you. Be humble enough to come to someone who has been authorised to teach people good manners.

بِسْمِ اللهِ الرَّحْمٰنِ الرَّحِيمِ

GIVE YOUR HAND TO CHARITY, YOUR SOUL TO THE LORD

We have been given a part of His Divine Presence, of His Divine Soul, which no other creature has, and have been created in a perfect way for a reason. Just like the earth has been created for a purpose. The sun was created for a reason. The moon was created for a purpose. Every creature has been created for a purpose. We look around and try to find out in which way we can use them.

We realise that we are the owners of this earth, we know that no other creature can reach this capacity and authority. There are so many creatures which are much more powerful than man, but they cannot control anything. You can control everything on earth. You can reach the deepest ocean. You can go to the skies and above. It is this kind of authority which makes you different from anything else around you. We try to find out the use of all creatures, except our own. Mankind does not bother to find out what their real reason for existing is.

We are at the end of this century, reaching out to the second millennium. Still man is occupied with their physical being, putting their full interest into their material world, even though they are aware of the fact that their material being will be put to an end by death. No-one lives on earth forever. We see thousands of people leaving this world every day. We see dead bodies being taken to the cemetery and put under ground, but we don't really ask what has happened. How is it possible that this body was still running around yesterday and today it can't? Why are we alive one moment and dead the next? Maybe the question comes to some people's mind, but they do not persist in trying to find out.

Since the beginning of life on earth Holy Books have been given to us. Man has always wanted to know what happens after death. But our educational systems today teach us nothing but theories about the beginning of life, and nothing about what happens after death. Science cannot bring contentment to people concerning the origins our their future. When someone today talks about death or beyond death, people are so embarrassed that they try to make a joke about it, or even worse, a taboo. It is very difficult today to speak about anything concerning Holy Books, people say these are bygone tales. But the situation of mankind is getting worse, because man needs to believe.

Beliefs make a person perfect. Man cannot be perfect without a belief. A person without a belief is a terrible person, more violent than a tiger, bear or wolf. From day to day the violence on earth is increasing.

Everybody is afraid of the coming days. Everyone is wondering what the coming millennium will bring. If they are not controlled, the competition between scientists, nations and weapon producers will increase to the point of explosion. Governments are spending 99% of their budget on weapons. What are they competing for? It is according to our violence. It is what our egos are asking for. They think that the most violent one will be the hero. We have not been sent to this life to kill, but to live. But the whole world now is intent on killing. All Holy Books: the Old Testament, the New Testament and the Last Testament, the Holy Quran, mention that when the Last Days approach, violence, killings and wars will increase. People will kill and be killed without knowing why.

We are like flocks, whatever our shepherds want us to do, we do. The reason that they can do with us what they want, is that our belief has reached the point of zero. This is what they want: they want us not to believe in anything. They want us to forget our Lord. The whole world is on the point now of not wanting to know anything about their Creator and not to believe, even though we need it. Even the biggest opponent of religions will start crying when he dies: Oh my Creator, oh Allah!

Since 60 years I am urging people to believe in their Creator. We believe that all prophets came as messengers from Heaven. Everyone of them brought a message from Heaven. The Lord of Heavens asked mankind to live happily and peacefully. The first man was created in

Paradise. The Lord of Heavens would have left them to live in Paradise forever, if satan, who was the first jealous one of all creation, had not wanted this high honour, which we have been given, for himself. When the Lord created us as his Deputies, satan was so angry and so jealous that he started chasing the first couple out of Peaceland, out of Paradise. This is why we were thrown out. He will never let us be in peace. But the Lord of Heavens has sent 124,000 prophets, all of them with messages to guide people to a happy peaceful life. Satan wants people to fall into troubles, miseries and sufferings.

Unfortunately everything in our days from east to west and from north to south, is turning in the wrong direction, is running after satanic ideas. The Heavenly Message has been thrown away. People are listening to satan and are making 'isms', 'isms', 'isms': communism, capitalism, feminism, kamalism... all of them are false. They are against the Divine Message. These are satanic ideas, his representatives have introduced them to throw people into misery.

We are reaching the second millennium. What is going to happen? If we do not change our direction, no doubt it will be terrible. There will be no more living people on earth. The majority will be killed and all buildings will be in ruins. Satan will sit on the mountain of ashes and be so happy: "Finally I have given my revenge to mankind!"

We have to see if we can save ourselves from that catastrophe. The Holy Books tell us that there will be a group of people who, even if everything else is going in the wrong direction, will go in the right. Moses* was a great prophet, he was the one who spoke with the Lord. Before his prophecy, when he was escaping from Egypt he came to the country of Kaana. He met Shuayb* (the Prophet Jethro) and promised to be the shepherd of his flocks for 7 years in return for marrying one of his daughters. This was his dowry. It is not permitted to marry anyone without a dowry. It can be anything, but the more you give, the more she will love you.

One day Moses* was with his flock in a valley full of wild animals. If he had just looked away for a second, they could have been attacked. It is very important to protect that which has been given to you as a trust. Suddenly he was overcome by heavy sleep, unable to open his eyes or even to stand up. At the same time he knew, that if he would fall asleep, at least half of his flock would be gone. If he would just be able to keep his eyes open, it would be enough, because the power of man lies in his eyes. So he said, "Oh my Lord, here is your servant. Your Will is above mine, it must continue..." with that he fell down, but within an instant he regained his strength. As he stood up he saw that the biggest of all wolves was standing above the flock keeping control over them and chasing away all the other wolves. The Lord addressed him, " Oh Moses*, you are what I want you to be. When you are with me, I am with you. I am looking after your flock. I can even make the wolf to be the shepherd over your flock!"

Try to be with Him and He will be with you. If a flood comes, like at the time of Noah*, you will be in safety. No titles which you carry in this life will be of any importance or any kind of life-style. I am teaching you the most honourable style in this life which will make you happy, successful, victorious, in safety and in peace. It is not important if you are a Muslim, a Jew, or a Christian. My advice for you, is to be with your Lord, and He is one.

Don't think that Christians have one Lord, Jews another, Muslims another. No! Be for Him. Be for Allah and you will be happy here and in the hereafter. Do your best for people. That will make you enjoyful always. Try to give your hand to charity and your soul to your Lord.

بِسْمِ اللَّهِ الرَّحْمَنِ الرَّحِيمِ

LEAVING TIME AND SPACE

Today is one situation, yesterday was another one. What you find today you will not have tomorrow. A beloved servant of Allah is one who agrees to every change in his own life and in others. It is a high rank of a believer to be happy and glad with every change without objection. Worshipping is easy. So many people pray. But to be happy with the Will of Allah the Almighty is not something everyone can do. Everyone knows this, but they do not practise it. When it would be necessary for them to do it, they are unable.

Allah is pleased with you when you are pleased with Him. If everything would be like the servant wants it to be, the servant would be happy. But on the contrary, if something happens which he is not prepared for, he will not be happy with His Lord. He will force himself to worship, and Allah doesn't like that. He wants us to worship with love and respect. I am not expecting you do to this at once, but step by step you can practise. You need endurance for every expensive target you want to reach.

We know our target and must try to reach it step by step. Even when we are in a plane we are informed of how we are getting higher and higher. We do not shoot up straight from the runway to the highest position. It is difficult to be patient, but we must, especially in our days.

Patience is the main means for an opening to Heavens, to be taken out of time and space. Before you leave time and space you must carry a heavy burden. Like a rocket before it reaches its orbit it needs huge powers. When it has reached its orbit it doesn't need anything. There gravity is finished. When we control our physical desires we can use our powers to take us out of the gravity of our egos and we will reach our orbits in Heaven.

بِسْمِ اللّٰهِ الرَّحْمٰنِ الرَّحِيْمِ

SUFI TARIQATS: THE WINGS OF ISLAM

We have two powers, one is a part of our physical body, the second is our spiritual being. The physical being uses batteries. When it eats and drinks it gets power. The second one does not need to eat or to drink. It works through Heavenly Power. Angels do not eat, drink or sleep, and still they never get tired. That kind of power comes to people through *zikr*. The more *zikr* you do, the more power you will get from Heaven. Step by step such a person will not need to eat, drink or sleep. Angels have been glorifying the Creator since beginning of time without ever stopping. They have been doing this for billions and trillions of years without tiring. People nowadays have lost that source of power. They want to get their power from eating and drinking. They eat vitamins, elixirs... They exercise and think they are becoming powerful! They are not. As long as they are not interested in their spirituality all that is rubbish! All animals are more powerful than those kind of people. Mankind have lost their way. They are going in the wrong direction. If they would know the real source, if they would keep the right direction, their lives would be so easy, peaceful, enjoyful and happy.

The handful of people who are interested in spirituality are not enough for mankind. The majority of people are on the level of animals. Their only interest is how they should eat, drink, dress and enjoy themselves. If anyone wants to reach their spiritual powers, the only way is to make *zikr*, to invoke the Name of the Lord constantly. This will bring them into the Divine Presence.

WELCOME TO HEAVENLY WAYS!

The Lord of Heavens asks us to sacrifice. It is most important that we try to sacrifice step by step. If you start leaving your physical desires you begin to sacrifice. If you attend to your spiritual desires more than to your physical, you are following the Ways of Heavens. Whoever wants to do that is welcome! It will not cost you anything. I will be paid by my Lord.

THE WAY TO PERFECTION

We are living for Allah. We hope to die for Him. A good life is to live for Allah, to be for Allah and to die for Allah. When you are living to be for Allah. When you are leaving, to leave for Allah. This is how Muslims should be.

Everything Muslims do should be for the pleasure of Allah. They shouldn't ask if people will be pleased or not. Only ask if Allah will be pleased. Don't expect when you give people charity or hospitality to get anything in return. Even if they deal with you in a bad way, don't be offended. You did it for Allah, not for man. You are looking after the servants of Allah. It is only Allah you want to please.

If you give people charities and they come against you, don't be sad. We have a saying: give charity and throw it to the sea. Like taking a dry piece of bread and throwing it into the sea. Fish will come and eat it without even knowing about you. They don't know who gave them this charity, but the Creator knows. Do everything for Allah. Never expect thanks from others. Like the fish. You will not be sorry. That is a high quality, not everyone can do it. Those who are being trained in a *tariqat* are like wild trees, or wild creatures living in the jungle. The perfection of man is not easily attained. After the first 40 days of pregnancy the embryo will take the form of a human, even if it is still very small. Allah the Almighty gives us the best of forms within 40 days, but the real perfection will come through the meaning you represent. That is not easy, it might take 40 years or more. It is not something you can learn in the university. No academy or university in our days can teach you that perfection. It can give you skills to control everything around yourselves, but it does not give you anything to control yourselves. If you cannot control yourself you are not a perfect one.

This is why we need another kind of training: associations with prophets, they are the first ones to train people on the way of perfection, to enable them to control themselves. If not, people will continue the way they have been born: wild. They will live in a wild way and die in the same way.

Wild people are not able to control their egos. Their egos bring every kind of violence to this world: fighting, troubles, problems, crisis... All of this is a result of the violence of people. It continues, it increases and perfect people are becoming more and more rare. There are thousands of people in the universities, but most of them are wild.

بِسْمِ اللهِ الرَّحْمٰنِ الرَّحِيمِ

THE SWEETNESS OF LIFE REVERSED

It has been granted to the *Umma-tul-Muhammad** that if something is difficult, beyond their capacity, power or ability, and they feel weak, to use the Holy Words, "*La* *haula wa la quata ila biLlah ilathi lathim*". These are Sacred Words. If someone is saying this out of their heart, they can move mountains and continents. That is how big the power is. Use it 100 times everyday! If there is something you are unable to carry, say, "*BismiLlahi rahmani rahim, la haula wa la quata ila biLlah ilathi lathim.*" and you will be able to carry it.

Life of man in these days is very heavy. It is most difficult. Never before has there been such a hard time for mankind. Technology has reached the top point. Machines are doing everything man used to. In spite of all inventions and instruments which have been made to ease the life of man in his everyday life, he has more problems than ever.

The physical body is now at rest, but spiritually people are falling apart and suffering. If someone is spiritually restless, their life will be like in hell. What help can all the machines be to him, if he has no satisfaction within himself? What can a car, ship, plane, TV or computer give me, if I am not at peace? Nothing! Billions in money, gold or jewels... What can it give me? If a lady becomes ill and is told that she has cancer, do you think that technology will take away her sadness? If all the jewels in the world were given to her, she would still not be happy. The 20th century is the most difficult time for mankind, even though we can do everything by just pressing a button. We have no taste of life. The taste of life comes from faith. When someone has lost that, there will be no taste. For example tea: you can drink it, but without sugar, it will be tasteless. If you add sugar it will get taste.

People are taking away faith from their life. So how do they expect a sweet life? Instead of putting sugar into it, they are adding poison, making it bitter, a bad bitterness.

They are not using the honey of faith. They have either lost it or thrown it away, saying that it is useless. Instead they take poison. This is why it is the most difficult time for mankind since the beginning of time.

Last night people were running until morning to find the sweetness of life. Do you think they found it? They want it so much, but they cannot reach it even though they run through the streets, into night-clubs, discos, theatres, cinemas, casinos... Don't think that they are tasting anything. All they are doing is getting the taste of poison. Don't be cheated by their clothes, jewels, cars, business, wealth, ranks, palaces, private lives, or the fact that they are so successful with young girls. There are so many things which can be added to the list of poisons. From the outside your ego might tell you that these people are tasting the taste of life, but they would love to get out. They just don't know how to do it. This is what Muhammad* was saying about the Anti-Christ, "He will demonstrate Paradise and hell. That which looks like Paradise will be hell, and his hell is in reality Paradise."

All these things; night-clubs, discos, bars, casinos, theatres, operas... are what the 30 small Anti-Christs are organising before the big Anti-Christ comes. They have given their worst to mankind by giving them this kind of life-style. They have formed a group of Anti-Christs who are above other people. These are the ones who are arranging the life-style of the young people. They are the ones programming the life of mankind now. All this has been programmed. They say, "If you pass through our programme, you will be in Paradise!".

Look at the life-style of the young ones everywhere! The Anti-Christ is dictating everyone; how they should live, what they should use, how to cook, how to eat, how to deal... everything has been programmed by the Anti-Christ. They are calling this paradise. In the universities everything is being programmed for them. Can you find anyone there with good behaviour? People are being turned into wild animals, planned by the Anti-Christ. "You must walk like this! You must do this! In your homes do this!"

Buildings, decorations, houses, clothes... everything must be programmed by them. "Don't eat all together! Eat like dogs: just take a bone and run away!" It is programmed and ordered. Everything is organised and programmed by the Anti-Christ, telling you that this is Paradise. "Oh people, your Paradise is here! If you talk to young people about Paradise and hell, they will tell you that is here. That if you have money you are in Paradise, and if you have no money, in hell. That is their life philosophy. This is a greater *fitna* than ever before. These Anti-Christs couldn't enter the homes of the 19th century, even though they started. Now they have invaded every place; the streets, the homes. They are programming and people are following.

"La haula wa la quata ila biLlah ilathi lathim!" This is why a believer must say this sentence a 100 times everyday to be able to carry the heavy burden of this life. Blessed are those who follow the Programme of Allah the Almighty. He is programming our lives, but we are refusing. Instead satan and the Anti-Christ program our life-style. We are running to them, leaving the life-style of Allah behind.

Do you think there is any hope for people like that? They must be taken away. If a tree is dry it has to be cut. In the same way: if an olive is dry and no good, it has to be thrown away. When it has been removed, the rest can grow again. All of these evil people have to go. Out of 7 people, 6 will go. You must run to Allah! Whatever He has programmed for you, do it! We must change our life and use His Programme everywhere. *"La haula wa la quata ila biLlah ilathi lathim."*

ALLAH ORGANISES EVERY ONE'S PROVISION

No-one can eat the provision of the other. No-one can die without finishing his provision. Your children come with their own provision, they do not come and start taking yours. This is a big misunderstanding. Allah the Almighty tells His servants not to worry about their provision. He tells us that He is providing for us daily. "I am not asking you to give me tomorrow's prayer today, but you want to have tomorrow's provision today! Or the provision of a week, a month, a year or a lifetime!" Why don't you ask cats and dogs how they survive? Do they have a trade, a garden or fields? Are they hunting? Do they do any work? Do they have shops, or businesses? Nothing, they have nothing! You are not surprised that they survive? So why do you ask me? If anyone starts doubting their provision, it means that they are doubting Allah's capacity of providing for everyone.

There are 100 people here. All of them have been sent by Him. He has organised for their provision to be here. Everyone takes their own share. Muhammad* used to say that a meal which has been prepared for 2 people is enough for 4 people. A meal for 4 will be enough for 8. If you prepare for 10 you will have enough for 20. Allah gives more *barakat* the more people come. A host must never be ashamed thinking that he cannot give enough to his guests. It is true that he cannot, but Allah can reach out to all his servants.

BOSNIA: AT THE TIME OF THE OTTOMANS THERE WAS PEACE IN THIS REGION!

This area used to be under Ottoman rule. It took more than military know-how to be able to conquer such a place, it took spiritual power. On the eve of the conquest in 1463 Sultan Mehmed Fatih was very worried, because he was not sure that Islam would be able to stay there forever. The next morning, however, he was full of certainty. When asked why, he told his people that Prophet Muhammad* had appeared in front of him and reassured him of success.

Wherever you go here you see Muslim cemeteries, which is a proof of this being a Muslim area. The Ottomans ruled here for 500 years, and this was only possible because they were just. We have to be aware of this even though neither the Europeans, nor the Turks want it to be Muslim. The Bosnians themselves lean on their Ottoman tradition and show the Ottoman flag everywhere! If they did that in Turkey, they would be arrested. The Muslim countries which are being ruled by the *Wahabis* also do not want Islam here, nor does Iran. Libya doesn't know what it wants. During the time of Ottoman rule, this area was peaceful.

In the course of centuries the Jewish people were longing for their own state. Within this plan the Sultan, as was monarchy, was in their way, because Palestine was a part of the Ottoman Empire. So democracy was invented: "Why should only one rule? That is not just! Power is for everyone!" Parties were formed: the party of the jackals, the party of the wolves, the party of the foxes, the party of the scorpions... a party of the rats was also formed, which was especially dangerous because it attacked from underneath. The different groups of people were incited against each other: "You are someone better because you are a Serb. You are Croatian. You are Pomak..." Where people had been living peacefully they were now starting to say, "This is my mountain, here is the border..."

Until then nationalism had not existed in the Ottoman Empire. The different groups were self administrated and had different tasks within the running of the Empire. The majority of the Wezirs, the ministers, came from Bosnia. But the more nationalism increased and the Ottoman Empire started to collapse, the more the hate between the different people increased. The wolves, rats, scorpions and foxes all started to demand claims on different areas and to use military force to achieve their goals. This resulted in civilian wars and struggles in which much blood was spilt and whole peoples were extinguished, for example the Pomaks. Until then there had been peace in the Balkans.

The jackals, wolves and other beasts wanted to have power for themselves, and the lion, who had ruled as their king until then, was in their way. They advised him to change his outer appearance completely and to modernise. He agreed. First they removed his beard. Then they wanted to give him new teeth, to make his face more beautiful. "Maybe you will not be able to chew for some time," he was told, "but don't worry, we will bring you soup!". The result of the operation was that the inside of his mouth resembled an empty cave. He was served the promised soup of snails which were filled with heroin and opium. He fell into a deep sleep during which his claws were cut. When he woke up a mirror was held up and he was told, "See how good you look. You are now a modern lion!" The poor lion was put out on show in the market square. Soon afterwards he died of shame and grief. Instead of burying him, he was just left to lie there. When the vultures were finished with him, only the bones remained and these can now be seen for a fee in a museum.

The Jews are now also divided. The discord they spread they now have in their own land. The Conservatives are against the progressives. Some American Jews do not even want to recognise the State of Israel. It is impossible to drive Islam out of Bosnia. Muslims are not only here in Bosnia, but in Sancak, Makedonia, Kosova, Bulgaria and Greece. They will unite and be stronger than before. They will call the Sultan and go with him to Istanbul. He will win. There will not be many losses on the side of the Bosnians. By the end of this century monarchy will be on its way, it will have strong roots. Oligarchy is finished. What is sown will bear fruits. No-one can change that. Monarchy brings people together, democracy makes people ill and envious. The devil wants to divide us. Parties divide people and create chaos. A Sultan unites the community.

ADVICE FOR THE BALKANS

The Grandmufti of Kosova told us that there is a massacre in his country without a reason. I cannot accept this. There is a reason: they are Muslims. People came there with a cross and asked the inhabitants to save their soul.

I was very pleased to hear from his Excellency the President of Chechnya that when he heard about the massacres in Kosova he was the first one who wanted to go there and to fight! His name is Aslan, which means lion. The Russians sent 1/2 million fully armed soldiers to Chechnya with a population of 2 1/2 million. The people of Chechnya said that they would face this army with their faith, because they are grandsons of lions like Imam Shamil. The people of Chechnya all belong to *tariqat*, they won their independence through, "*La illaha illaLlah*".

The Muslims of the Balkan were under communism for a long time and they lost their *tariqats*. They need *tariqats* and *zikr*, that is what will give power to their hearts. They are now loving this world more than Allah and are unable to give their souls for the sake of Allah. The Russians signed the independence of Chechnya because their armies were moving with, "*La illaha illaLlah*", "*La illaha illaLlah*", "*La illaha illaLlah*".

This is what I am advising the people of the Balkans to do. They left the spiritual path and a curse came on them. Let them open their *tekkes*, their *zawiyas* and their *derghas* and follow the command of Allah and do *zikr*.

WAKE UP! THE WORLD IS BURNING!

Every religion comes to establish peace on earth. I am trying to give people peace. Satan wants the opposite: to establish war. When people follow satan their struggles are neverending. When they follow prophets and the Holy Commands of Allah, they will reach peace. In this century we need peace more than anything else. Everywhere there is the fire of fighting. The world is burning. There is fighting in the street, in the school, in the office, in business, in homes, amongst young ones, amongst rich ones, amongst citizens, amongst village people... Nations are struggling within themselves and against others. There is no peace now. I do not think that your Creator, the Lord of Heavens, wants you to fight. Stop fighting and start to listen to the Commands of Heavens! It is because you are not hearing, listening and obeying the Holy Commands of Heavens that suffering, miseries and troubles are increasing. There are endless troubles without a solution. If you try to bring a solution to a problem, you will find 10 new problems. If you solve them you will find 100. Why? Does Christianity tell you to fight? Did Jesus Christ* advise Christians to fight? Did Moses* tell his people to fight against each other? Did Muhammad*? Is there any religion which is telling us to fight?

Satan causes us to oppose each other. He gives us all these reasons. He says it is an economical problem. That is the biggest lie! He is the biggest cheater. It is not an economical problem. The disaster is that people are not finding out about the Holy Commands of Heavens, so without even knowing it, they are disobedient. That causes the biggest problem.

People have never been as rich as they are in our times. Muhammad* told us that there will come a time when money will come in abundance. 60 or 70 years ago people were working for so little money. A worker would work from sunrise to sunset for 3 piaster and it was enough to feed a family. Now the money in Turkey is worth so little that even young boys are millionaires. People in these days have so much money, but they are not satisfied. People are millionaires, billionaires, trillionaires They are so rich! Markets are full of everything. Still we are being told that it is an economical crisis. There are some huge companies who take all the gold and put it underground. Then they give us paper money. On it they write £1.-, $10.-, DM 100.-, but it is only paper. The real value, gold, is kept underground. Then they create the stock market so that they can play with the money. "Keep it! Sell it! Buy it!..." They are behaving like people from the mental house. Every country has a central bank, even Saudi Arabia. When they had their first king, they were not using this kind of money. King Abdul Aziz was only using silver coins. After him everything was changed, and his learned people did not object.

Our *Shariah* tells us that we cannot buy anything with paper, because you can cut it and throw it away. It is worthless: you can put it in water and it will melt. You may put it in fire and it will burn. The *Shariah* does not allow us to buy or sell with something which has no value. People should use something valuable for trade. But people are keen to do everything which is against the Divine Rules. This is why we have all these troubles. In the last years money has even been changed into plastic cards. Representatives of satan want to control everything, Christians are sleeping, Muslims are sleeping, but some people are waking up. Christians have been given one tablet of valium, Muslims ten! Muslims are like cows, full of milk!

Don't blame other people. Open up your own eyes. What did Allah the Almighty say to you, to Muslims to Christians and to Jews? You must follow these rules! Since 60 years I am fighting against demons. They never like me. They are my first class enemies. I hate evil. Devils and evil are destroying everything on earth. Satan has established his kingdom and I want to wake up people to be against him. I would like to continue on this way until I leave this life. I would like to be in the Divine Presence of the Lord and still be against the sultanate of the devil.

One cigarette already supports his kingdom. Did you know that? It is a very simple example which will wake you up. People are burning trillions of dollars for that every day. All for the honour of satan, or did you think they are doing it for Allah? Then they cry about an economical crisis. If they would just stop smoking for one day, it would finish every economical crisis in the world. What can we say?

I am nearly eighty years old, but I have come here to establish a group of people against the sultanate of satan, Muslims, Christians, Jews... any kind of people. All prophets came to destroy the satanic kingdom on earth. But people never supported prophets, the majority supported satan.

This is why Allah sent His Heavenly Curse to destroy people. I am afraid now, because once more most people are supporting satan. A Divine Curse will come on them and destroy billions, like it is mentioned in all Holy Books as Armageddon, the biggest war which will be on earth before the last day. It will be a Heavenly Curse for the people of the 20th century because they supported satan during the whole of this century. They lived for satan and they died for satan. But we have been ordered to live for Allah and to die for Allah.

THE ISLAMIC FLAG HAS NO SWORD

Why have the Saudis put a sword on their flag? The Islamic flag should have *"La illaha il'la'Llah, Muhammad rasul Allah"* written on it, not a sword! They only do this to make people fear Islam. Why? We do not accept it! Put a crescent in the four corners, the moon and a star. But not a sword! They want others to say that we want to force them with the sword, that Islam is spread by the sword. That is what they claim, and say that Christianity has no sword. Even though Christians are using every kind of weapon. At the same time they blame us for using a sword. Yes, in the beginning the followers of Jesus Christ* did not use swords, but then they started to use anything to kill people. This is important to know.

THE HOLY QURAN, NOT A MIND-PRODUCTION !

His Guidance is for every nation. Even though our mother-tongue is not Arabic, Allah the Almighty makes it possible for every one of us to recite the Holy Quran in the same way as Arabs do. This is a grant from Allah the Almighty for all nations. It is a blessing. Another endless Favour of His, is that Muslims are able to memorise the verses of the Holy Quran. It is impossible for any other nation to be able to recite their Holy Book without looking at it. At every Christian or Jewish ceremony, they will always look at their book to be able to read it. These books haven't entered their hearts. If something is not engraved in your heart, you cannot know it by heart.

It is a miracle when a ten year old boy is able to memorise the whole Holy Quran, to keep it in his heart and to be able to recite it from beginning to end. If it isn't a Holy Book, how would this be possible? Most people who know the Quran by heart are not Arabs. 6666 verses! 114 *suras*! Ordinary people even have a hard time memorising the titles of the suras.

Why haven't the Christians started to look yet? Their Bishops, or even the Pope, or the Patriarch in Turkey should start to read it. Even if they would only read two lines, it would prove to them that the Holy Quran is from Heavens, not the words of a man, of a prophet. I was in Germany last year when an old person came to me who was an editor and a poet. He brought me a book which contained poems he had written. He opened the book and started to read one. I told him to close the book and to continue to read. He couldn't, even though he had written it himself.

How is it possible that people cannot see the miracle of Muhammad*, an illiterate person being able to recite 600 pages, 6666 verses by heart? He never went to school, he never learned how to read or write, still people insist that the Holy Quran was written by him! If he had written it himself, would he have been able to know it by heart? Any other book which is learned by heart would be changed every time you try to recite it again. It would be changed again and again, and after ten times never be the same as the original again.

How is it possible that Sayyidina Muhammad* would recite it the same way as it was given it the Archangel Gabriel? Oh Christians, oh Jews, oh unbelievers, you must know that the Holy Quran is not a mind production! It was sent by the Lord through the Archangel Gabriel to His Last Messenger.

TRUTH HAS THE POWER TO TOUCH YOUR HEART

Every night you can see the shining planet of Venus and the moon. If you claim to see someone clearly on Venus, but not to see a thing on the moon, can that be accepted by positive knowledge?

How is it possible that people see more clarity in Jesus Christ* who was 2000 years ago, when everything they know has been passed on to them through books? Why would the knowledge of another miraculous person, which has been brought to them in the same way, be ignored? Did their books come from Heavens, or were they written by men? Were the Gospels written by angels without a mistake? Can the mind accept why one is acceptable and the other one isn't?

We believe in Jesus*, in Moses*, in the Old Testament and the New Testament without losing our faith. But they say, that if they would believe in Muhammad* they would lose their faith. Why? Jewish people refuse both: Jesus Christ* and Sayyidina Muhammad*? What was wrong with Jesus Christ*? He was from their tribe, he was from the Children of Israel, he was a practising Jew! Why did the Jews attack him? They are still refusing him! What was wrong with Muhammad*? Why are they fighting against him? There is no reason. They are accepting all prophets, except Jesus Christ* and Sayyidina Muhammad*!

Christians are accepting all prophets, including Moses* and the Old Testament, but they are refusing Sayyidina Muhammad*. What is the reason? Muhammad* called Moses* the Word of Allah and accepted the *Thora*. He also respected all other prophets, telling his people to believe in them. But neither Christians nor Jews respect our religion.

If Allah will give a judgement to all of this, what would it be? Would He say that they gave their best? If you refuse someone who is respecting you? This is why the power of Christianity has stopped. It cannot give any spirituality to the hearts of people.

On my way from Barcelona to here, there were so many monasteries. But they are empty, they are dead monasteries. Even the churches are for sale. What does it mean? People are not interested. Many new villages in Europe are now being built without churches. People go to cathedrals like they go to museums: to see old paintings. That is not what it was meant for. But still the heads of Christianity are not accepting Islam as a religion, as part of the same religion! It doesn't matter. If anyone wants to accept that Muhammad* is a Prophet of Allah, or not, is up to them. To be in safety you must accept all. If a Christian or Jew now says, "*La illa'ha il la'Llah, Muhammadu rasul Allah*" and becomes a Muslim, he will neither lose his Christianity nor the fact that he is from the tribe of Moses. We are not disputing that Jesus* is the spirit of Allah, nor that Moses* represents the Word of Allah. We are only saying, that you should also believe that Muhammad* is a messenger of Allah too.

بِسْمِ اللَّهِ الرَّحْمَنِ الرَّحِيمِ

PEOPLE OF THE HOLY BOOKS ALL KNEW THAT THE LAST PROPHET WOULD COME FROM ARABIA

The area of the Arabian Peninsula is the main source of Divine Revelation. No prophet has ever been mentioned having come from Europe: Germany, France or Spain! All prophets came from Palestine, from Mesopotamia, from the Arabian Peninsula. All Holy Books: the Old

Testament, the New Testament and the Quran, mention Prophets coming from that area, not from here, from Europe, from Africa or from America. In the old days the big spiritual centres of Christianity, monasteries and churches, were concentrated in the area of Palestine. They were expecting Heavenly Revelations and were finding that the sources of spiritual power were in that area.

Once an Emir of Medina passed through Damascus. They came to a monastery but the doors of the main entrance were closed. They knocked, knowing that someone must be there. They waited for a long time, because Allah orders that if anyone comes to a place, they must ask permission from the owner to enter. It is prohibited to enter some one's property by force. Even the sultan cannot do that. This man had come on the orders of the sultan. He was waiting for them to ask him to enter. That is real Islam. You cannot find it anymore. Just like you cannot find real Christianity or real Judaism.

After a while the abbot opened the door and they entered. The chief of the sultan's caravan asked why they had to wait, and they were told, "We apologise for the delay, but we have read in our Holy Books that if you are afraid of someone, you should make ablution and then welcome them. We saw that you are the caravan of the sultan, this is why we asked everyone to wash themselves. After the ablution we did our prayer and now we are under the protection of the Lord. You will not be able to harm us."

People now know nothing about real Christianity. The people in the monasteries in those days were reading their Holy Books and practising. This is why they were so different to the people living now. *Wudu*, ablution, protects people from devils and his representatives. All Holy Books of Christians and Jews demand their followers to do ablution every day before every prayer, for every occasion. *Wudu* is a strong weapon against satan. Satan cannot touch a clean person.

All these monasteries which have spread in the Arabian Peninsula were not there without a reason. Their Holy Books had mentioned that the Last Messenger would come from Arabia. The Christians were expecting the last messenger to come in the Yemen, to the Kingdom of Aden. People in Damascus were expecting the Last Messenger in Arabia, and the Jews were expecting and waiting for the Last Messenger to come in Medina, where the Prophet's tomb is now. They all knew that the Last Prophet would be coming from Arabia.

The Last Prophet was not a surprise, he was expected. When he came some people recognised him, others didn't. Most Christian priests and monks came and accepted him. So many of the Jewish rabbis also came and recognised him as the one who had been foretold. But many denied him without having any evidence. The greatest proof that he was not just an ordinary person, is the fact that 1 1/2 billion people are now following him and are saying, "*La illa'ha il la'Llah, Muhammadur rasul Allah*".

This is knowledge from Holy Books, I am not saying this from myself, I am saying it from my heart.

EATING PLASTIC CANNOT FILL YOU

If He wanted to make every person the same, He could. Like in a factory: all the same form, colour and size, and everyone speaking the same language. But Allah the Almighty didn't. You cannot find two identical people. Everyone is unique in their creation. Allah does not need to make copies of people. Everyone is different, but all belong to the same mankind.

Everything is created in a different way. Even a grain of corn is not identical to another, or a grain of wheat. You must try to get to know His greatness and power! Everything which is part of Him is without limit. His existence is unlimited from pre-eternity until eternity. He is the First and He is the Last. Do you think He was starting to feel old and therefore needed a son? He exists from pre-eternity to eternity. That does not mean that He was young during pre-eternity and then became old during eternity so that He felt a need to create a crown prince as a successor! It is impossible.

The people of the 20th century are not using their mentality and their mind, so they attack Islam. Even though Islam brought the perfect description of the Lord, Almighty Allah. I am angry. Why? Last week I was in the cathedral built in the grand mosque of Cordoba. It is full of imagination. They picture an old man sitting. To his right hand there is a young person, at the other a lady. That is a creation of their imagination. They want us to believe that the old one is the Lord, who has taken the young one from earth to sit next to him. I feel so ashamed. The Christians are to blame for this. They have created it and they believe in it.

We are living in the 20th century. Within this huge universe we are like an atom. When we look amongst ourselves we see different kinds of people, of all sizes but never bigger than 3 meters. Do you think that even a huge person like that would be able to create such a huge universe, and then be able to die? How could Christianity develop in this way? Are these the teachings of Jesus Christ*?

All prophets, including Jesus Christ*, brought real descriptions of the Creator. But there are people who have changed the originality of Christianity. They exchanged every truth with plastic. This is why Christianity does not give satisfaction to the souls of people. It is impossible when you eat plastic food to be full. That is the real problem in this world at the moment. People are spiritually hungry, they want to be content and satisfied, but they cannot find it. If anyone asks for real food while they are being offered all this plastic, the sellers become very angry and will tell them, "Islam is not good!"

Have these people really tasted Islam before giving such a judgement? How can you judge something without knowing it or having tasted it? That is being prejudiced, which is a sin. It is a great lie to accuse someone of something without having proof. We look at the Old Testament and the New Testament, we are not afraid of doing that, but Christians are not allowed to read the Holy Quran in their churches. Why are they prevented from doing that? Read and comment! If you haven't read it, don't say anything. If you read and you don't understand, then ask those who do. A new millennium is approaching. Still Christians believe that the 21st century will be Christian. They say that Islam is out of time and not suitable for this age. Let them prove that Christianity is suitable!

Mankind has lost every value of being human. It has no value anymore, and Christians and Jews are inventing such terrible weapons which will destroy everything civilisation has built in thousands of years. Islam comes for peace, but the learned people within Christianity know very well that Islam is the last message which has come from Heavens to guide all nations.

بِسْمِ اللهِ الرَّحْمَنِ الرَّحِيمِ

SPAIN: ISLAM FROM WITHIN

One thousand years ago Islam came from the outside to Spain and then it was thrown out. Now Islam is coming back again. This time from the Spanish people themselves. You can tell the Muslims who have come from the outside to go back home again, because you are the hosts, the landlords of Spain. No-one can tell you to leave. They were Arabs who came here, and the Spanish Christians told them to go away. But the Lord is watching and is giving His Revenge. Your ancestors threw out the Muslims, but now their descendants are becoming Muslims. No-one can push you away. It is impossible. *Al hamdulillah!*

MAKE ISLAM EASY FOR BEGINNERS

Allah did not send the whole *Shariah* in one day. It was completed within 23 years. It shows us that the followers of Muhammad* were improving their prayers step by step. First they were only praying 2 rakats. After the Night-journey Allah ordered them to pray 5 times. We too must try to make the way easy for new Muslims.

HEAVENS IS RULED BY A KING, SO SHOULD WE

Centuries and millenniums change, but reality never will. The rules which the Creator has given us for this world never change from the beginning until the end. His Kingdom is absolute, no democracy or election can bring in this or that new suggestion! Kingdom is the best for mankind, because Heavens is ruled by a King, and so should we.

But satan puts the feet up and the head down. Mankind has lost their head and their feet since 1789, the foolish French Revolution, the biggest, dirtiest and most cruel one. Since then the power of satan has been spreading throughout the world. It has taken away the heads of every country and put feet in its place. That is democracy! There is no democracy in Islam. It is the biggest lie. We keep the rules of the Kingdom of Heavens. Kings cannot do as they like. They are under the control of the Heavenly King, they follow the Rules of Heavens. Those are real kings.

Muslims today need such a powerful sultan, who will be under the control of the Sultan of Heavens. We shouldn't be divided into Pakistan, Algeria, Palestine, Iraq, Syria, Turkey, Afghanistan, Iran, Saudi, Yemen, Egypt, Libya, Algeria, Morocco, Tunisia, Sudan, Albania... no! One king! Go and ask Allah at the Kaaba to send one king to the Muslims who has power to control all Muslims.

Look at what happened in China: one billion people were under the control of one person, Mao Tse Tung. Don't say that it is not possible, it is! There was an Italian who was feared by half the world. He was able to control the world from Siberia to Warsaw. Don't say that it is not possible for the big Muslim world to have one leader. It is, and it is necessary!

This is why we are in such a bad position, because we have put the head to the ground and the feet are on top. The Prophet* was saying, that this is a sign of the Last Days. Everyone wants to go the way they want, without a king to rule them. But He is the King of Judgement Day. He has never described Himself as being a president. He calls Himself the King of Judgement Day and the King of Kings.

Every Muslim should be aware of this reality. Allah the Almighty has made it obligatory for every believer, man and woman, to know about themselves and about their *umma*. This should be taught, learned and known. But the *umma* is asleep, satan has put us to sleep. We hope that there will be a big change for the benefit of believers. We will win and the others will lose, *insha'Allah*.

NO DIVINE LAWS WITHOUT A SULTAN

We need a Sultan. Without a Sultan we will not be able to defend ourselves in a Divine Way. There must be one Sultan for all Muslims. That is the Holy Command of Allah the Almighty. But people have lost it. 75 years ago the Turks threw away their Caliph, the Sultan. The ancestors of the Muslims of Hindistan helped to save the *Maqqam-ul-Khilafa*, the Sultan, but finally they were cheated. For 75 years now the Muslims have lost their Sultan. The *Shariah* cannot work without a Sultan, and a Sultan cannot work without the *Shariah*. One completes the other. You must always remind people of this. In 1999 it is the 700th anniversary of the beginning of the Ottoman Empire. We hope that Allah the Almighty will give them their power to be on the way of Islam as they were before.

SPIRITUAL MONARCHY

The English used to say that there were two kinds of people living in Cyprus: Muslims and Christians, not Greeks and Turks, but Muslims and Christians. All troubles of this century have been made dirty and so many wars have been fought in the name of nationalism. We have not been ordered to fight the *People of the Book*. Allah has granted them to be living with Muslims in the same villages and town without being attacked. Islam never touched them or harmed them.

When nationalism came all this changed. The same is happening on this island too: Scottish people are unhappy with English people, English people are unhappy with Scottish people. Irish people are unhappy with English people and the English people are unhappy with them too.

The same in France: the people in the North are unhappy with the South and the other way around. The West Germans are unhappy with the East Germans. The people in Singapore are unhappy with the people in Malaysia. The Malaysians are unhappy with the Indonesians and they are unhappy with Brunei and Brunei is unhappy with Singapore! Iraq is unhappy with Southern Iraq. The Syrians are unhappy with Lebanon. South Lebanon is unhappy with North Lebanon. North Turkey is unhappy with South Turkey... all these partitions give so much trouble. It is what satan is asking for. The Labour Party is unhappy with the Conservatives...

A wisdom tells us that a believer cannot make the same mistake twice by putting his finger into a hole. If he has done it once and a scorpion has bit him, he would not repeat it, unless there is something seriously wrong with him. How many times have the English people tried the Labour Party? Every time when they get angry with the Conservatives they do it again, even though the Labour Party will put them in a worse situation than the Conservatives did.

Neither the Conservatives nor the Labour Party will bring any solution, only a traditional Kingdom can. This applies to every country. Democracy is hypocrisy! Democracy is for you today, tomorrow for him... But the monarchy is there all the time, which is why they do not need to take as much as possible for themselves once they are in power. In a democracy the rulers will be changed so they will try to fill their pockets as much as possible. People are unhappy when I say this, but in a democracy you are allowed to say what you want. In a monarchy people will develop to their high positions, but in a democracy they will just be put there without having achieved anything. That is wrong. Kings and Caliphs have been trained all their lives for their position. But what can we say? They are advertising everywhere that democracy is good, but it isn't.

This is why Allah the Almighty is preparing the spirituality of the Caliphs and is making them much more powerful. The power of monarchy is in the hands of the sultan. He is responsible to protect the Divine Law here on earth. The spiritual leaders were more powerful than the sultan. If they said that he was not suitable for the *umma*, he would be taken away and killed. At the time of the Ottoman Empire this is how it was. If anyone tried to split up the Empire he would be killed.

It is mentioned in the Holy Quran that when the children of Israel were defeated by King Nebukhadnezzed and he destroyed the Temple of Jerusalem, they ran to the prophet of the time and said, "Oh Messenger of God, please ask The Almighty to send us a King!". They were not asking for a president! They wanted someone to be able to control the whole country and who could help them to win against the enemies. They were asking Allah to elect their leader, their king. That is how it is written in the Holy Book.

You cannot be like the rulers. He must be on top. The children of Israel went to their Prophet to ask for intercession. Why didn't they ask Allah directly? People have no mind. They are denying intercession. So many young people are asking, "What is a sheikh, what is *wasila*...? We must ask Allah directly..." Ask! And look if He will answer your prayer! Why does it say in the Quran that the Children of Israel went to their Prophet and asked him to ask Allah to send them a King, a Sultan. You are such weak people, heedless Muslims, too weak to follow that example. You go to the UN for Kashmere, to the UN for Cyprus, to the UN for Kosova, to the UN for Palestine... What is that? We should be ashamed that we are not asking the Prophet*. I am quoting the Quran, no-one can object on it. Allah is showing us the way for all problems. As long as we are not going to the Prophet* we will be going, coming, going, coming to the UN and waste a lot of shoes!

Let us ask the Prophet* to send us a Sultan. We hope that he is coming...

بِسْمِ اللّٰهِ الرَّحْمٰنِ الرَّحِيْمِ

THE END OF TECHNOLOGY

Rajab is a Holy Month and it is accompanied by Heavenly Powers. It brings us good news of Jesus*. He is requesting his declaration to be sent to the whole world: "The new millennium will be under my rule!" We have been informed of this by Muhammad* too. He told us that Jesus* will be on this earth for another 50 years. The time now until the year 2000 is a preparation for everyone to be woken up, for them to understand that the next millennium will belong to Jesus Christ*. He is informing us to pass this message on everywhere. None of the rubbish of this century, all these 'isms', first of all democracy, will be thrown away. Kings will come back. Many kings are ready in their countries, but their tongues and hands are tied. They are not allowed to speak. They have been imprisoned, but they will be freed by the Royal Kingdom of Jesus Christ*. This is why a new group is evolving until the coming of Jesus Christ*. He has asked them to be called the 'Legion of the Royal Kingdom of Jesus on earth'. He wants every real believer of Muslims and Christians to be servants of his Royal Kingdom, because it will be the Kingdom of Heavens on earth.

This is a very, very important message. Spread it from east to west to every nation. His power is descending now. The powers of evil and of the devils will decrease until it reaches zero. It is a countdown. Be alert, the seeds of goodness are increasing. This is *haqq*. Evil will disappear. Up to the year 2040 and then 2050 Jesus Christ* will be here and rule his Heavenly Kingdom according to His Heavenly Commands. He will clean everything on earth. *Mehdi* alehi salam will be with him for 7 years. Then he will pass on to Heavens. Jesus Christ* will pray the funeral prayer for him in Jerusalem.

Jesus Christ* will give the hidden powers of Heavens and of the Holy Quran to the people and spirituality will increase. People will be spiritual beings. Just like they are now mostly physical, they will be transformed 100% into spiritual beings. Luckiest are those who will be part of that time. Jesus Christ* will share his spirituality with all nations. Everyone will have miraculous powers.

Technology will be killed. The Anti Christ depends fully on technology with the aim of taking away all spirituality. That is why technology has to be stopped first. When that has been taken away, spirituality will appear. Now no-one can imagine the power of spirituality in comparison to technology. No-one will be interested in any technology! It will be put into the dustbin. Within one night all parts of technology will be collected by the *jinn*, put into a great sack and thrown out into space onto the heads of Gog and Magog! They will as usual expect it to be something to eat, because that is all they want. When they see the computers, TVs, fridges, washing machines, planes, cars and all that, even they will throw it away. They will be so upset by such a silly present, that they will want to come out of their prison to eat us raw. This is what is approaching. The whole world will be changed completely. Prepare yourselves! Don't waste your life!

I do not want to cheat you. I have been ordered to tell the truth. We are *haqqanis*. If someone is happy with that, I am also happy. If someone is unhappy, we can put a saddle on him... The people of the 20th century are so pleased when satan takes them for a ride. May Allah forgive us and bless you!

TECHNOLOGY ENVIES THE SOUL OF HUMANITY

All knowledge which has reached us in our days through technology, is changing the inner feelings of mankind. It is making them like robots, just moving by pressing a button and doing what they are being ordered to do. We have now reached the worst point of technology in the 20th century, and still mankind is most dangerously bowing to it! Humanity is dying because technology is ordering it to be killed. It wants it killed because humanity has value, which technology has not. Technology wants to take these values away.

Look after yourself and your Heavenly Souls! Don't be slaves of technology. It takes people to a point of not having any feelings. Having feelings is the speciality of being human. It is what gives us value in the Divine Presence. Servanthood is our highest rank and honour. We bow in His Divine Presence.

CLEANING UP

Our aim is to clean people in their minds, thoughts, knowledge, intentions, intelligence, hearts, bodies, works, beliefs and in their lives. We want to remove hatred, harm and hurt, and make them give their best to everyone. The majority of people are used to being heedless. Their lives are like the lives of those living in hell.

We want to clean the villages, towns, cities, countries and oceans. People are concerned about cleaning the oceans, but they do not do the same for mankind. They give the greatest importance to rid the seas of dirt, without considering that the cause of that dirt is a result of a dirty mankind. They only want to clean the ocean. It is impossible! If mankind continues to make the oceans dirty, what use is it? Satan and his companions benefit from the dirt of mankind and never want mankind to be clean. Their priority is to make mankind dirty all the time. The headquarters of satan is based in western countries, just like the American fleet is based in Malta, Ibiza... They are very welcome in these countries. No-one asks them for a passport, no visas... "Welcome to you! We are under your command!" They are treated 70 times better than any other VIPs. "This is your country! You do not need any work permit. You can work wherever you want!" I am against them, and I hope to remove them. One day our dream will become reality.

USEFUL AND USELESS EDUCATION

The devil tells you to study instead of working. He urges people to study. He never encourages them to learn a craft. Those who know a craft can live, others can't. The path of studying is closed. People who study want a job from the government, but the government cannot offer a job to every graduated student. The jobs are filled. They are now inventing so many useless offices and bureaucracy to be able to employ people. But it is impossible. Offices are like schools. Hundreds and thousands of people are coming out. You think it is another kind of university. They all come out with their Samsonite cases as a sign of their illness.

The devil tells you to go to university to make degrees. He urges young people to study. For what? You cannot employ them. They are like armies of graduated unemployed. There are two kinds of learning. One is useful, the other is useless. All universities are giving useless knowledge. They distribute diplomas which cannot be used. If they were useful, the young people would be able to be employed.

In Turkey there is an office in which they needed 50 or 60 employees. 4,000 people came to apply! They came there full of hope and went back hopeless. So many young people are committing suicide nowadays. Satan is very pleased. These young people are wasting their youth and reach nothing.

Everyone must learn a craft. I do not like people to go to university. They are being cheated by the devil. For young people it is like a picnic, a place for amusement. There are so many boys and girls there... It is like a discotheque where young people are learning everything except knowledge. There are so many things which the community would need. But pride does not let people learn such simple works. Another kind of habit for the family of girls is to ask a boy when he proposes to their daughter, "What is your profession? "

"I am a carpenter!"

"We want our daughter to marry a doctor or an engineer! Not a carpenter, a shoemaker, a greengrocer, a farmer, a shepherd or a factory worker!" The family of the boy will ask the same questions. They don't want old fashioned wives. Everywhere people are following the will of satan, which is why everything is going wrong. We must change, otherwise the direction which every country is taking, will be the end of humanity. Teach your children crafts which will benefit the community, not burden.

OLD PEOPLE AND YOUNG PEOPLE SHOULD MIX!

The Prophet David* said that from time to time old people have to be with young people. Their energies will be transferred and wake up their physical powers. If all old people just sit together they will get weaker and weaker and finish. This is why they must sometimes go and look at playing children.

At the same time it is just as useful for young people to learn from the old who have passed so many trials from which they can learn their lessons too. They cannot learn such experiences by themselves. These are very good lessons which cannot be learned anywhere else. They must go and visit old people sometimes and listen to what they have to say. When they are interested, the meeting will be fruitful.

If you are not interested in what I have to say, I will not speak. If you do not look after a tree, it will not flourish. Old people have so many experiences which they like to speak about. It will give them contentment, satisfaction and happiness by sharing it. Everyone has been given something from the Creator. Within a long life you learn so much, you pass so many bridges which youngsters haven't come to yet.

HIS SPECIALITIES

He speaks without needing a mouth, a tongue or teeth. He may do everything without needing anything. He can do everything as He likes. He has will power and it is not like ours. Each of His Attributes are endless, unlimited and never-ending. He can speak, listen, see and do. He has an endless will. Everything goes according to His Will, nothing is above it. These attributes are His Specialities. Through these main attributes endless specialities come. Only a little spot of that can be seen within all creatures, because He has endless existence and countless creatures, worlds, heavens and servants. This is why it is impossible to limit His Specialities.

Every perfection which appears within His creatures, is a speciality of the Lord of Heavens. You are appearing within all this and are witnessing a speciality of His Creation. One of His Attributes is to be able to create countless creatures. This speciality appears in His Creation. This is a short description of that which has reached us through Holy Books. When our Divine Knowledge improves, more and more grants from Heaven will appear to show you of His Existence and His Specialities.

A SNAKE CANNOT BE PACIFIED BY MERCY

Jesus Christ* will not come like he came the last time. He will come to kill the dragon because the world is now full of evil. The first time he came he showed his mercy, with the result that people came against him, wanting to kill him. This time his mission is to correct everything. You may pacify a cat by stroking him, but not a snake!

WHY WE LOSE OUR PEACE

People can more or less reach their desires through technology, but they are losing their inner peace, even though they are asking for real peace. I do not think that common people want to fight or to have wars. They want continuous peace. The way to peace passes through our inner peace. If you can reach peace within yourself, the community will reach peace and general peace will come. The way to reach this peace is to come to the level of simplicity.

PURE HEARTS

He, Who created and honoured mankind, wants them to be
friendly, help each other, support each other, love each
other, keep justice and the rights of each other. Even an ant
has rights. The smallest creatures have rights.

If Allah the Almighty does not give His Permission,
nothing can harm you or hurt you. But if you leave His
Divine Service and start hurting others, He will let them
hurt you. Even the smallest bacteria may kill you. It can
enter your body and develop into an army of bacteria. But
if you go on the right path and give the rights to the
Creator, He will keep you and protect you. Everything will
help you, and never harm you.

We are now in the 20th century. It is coming to an end
and we are entering into the 2 millennium. What are we
doing? We, these 6 or 7 billion people on earth? Are we
living for the service of the Lord or for satanic trips and
traps: harming each other and trying to kill masses of
people?

People are trying to kill millions in one go, destroying
everything which mankind has built since thousands of
years. Is that the civilisation you are so proud of? People
have become slaves of technology. They are not on their
knees in front of their Lord, but in front of technology,
handmade technology! The second millennium is coming
closer, and something else too: if we do not change our
attributes, a curse will come. No power on earth can stop

it. Everyday we see such terrible weapons on television which have been made by us, mankind, to kill each other. We are cursed because of that.

Allah will not punish His disobedient people in the way He did in the past. Some were punished by a flood, some by earthquakes, some by winds, some by fire... Different kinds of punishments befell the people, and they were taken away. This nation will not be punished from above, but from within themselves.

People are in different groups, in different camps, becoming enemies of each other and killing each other. That is the punishment this time. There is a traditional rule: the one who kills will go to hell and so will the one who is killed. The one who is killed was intending to kill, but the other one was quicker. People with bad intentions must be punished. Pure hearts never carry bad intentions. Pure hearts never carry jealousy. Pure hearts never carry enmity. Pure hearts never carry hatred. Pure hearts never intend to harm others. Pure hearts cannot be against other people. Pure hearted people live only for their Lord. Bad people do not live for their Lord. They live for the sake of this world.

All of us have different forms, races and colours. As I was praying I had a vision of a meadow. Do you think that a meadow consisting only of green grass would be better than one with different kinds of flowers in it? No doubt the flowered one! Have you seen different kinds of flowers living side by side? Have you ever seen the yellow flower fighting the red flower? There are so many different flowers living friendly side by side in the meadow. But you, mankind, are unable to see the reality of different races and sexes and nations. Why can't you see the harmony, peace and enjoyment? Why aren't you trying to make a peaceful world?

HOLY PEOPLE

People do not become holy because they are appointed by us. Real Holy People must be appointed by Heavens. Holiness is a grant from Heavens to people. You cannot give that title to anyone, only He can.

BLESSINGS

We ask for His Blessings. It gives us light, takes sadness away, gives refreshment, enjoyment, contentment and satisfaction to our hearts. Without His Blessings that is impossible. This is why you should ask at every occasions for His Blessings to make you happy and in peace. If blessings come on you, your dreams will also be pleasant. If not, they will be full of wolves, snakes, dragons and bad things. It is important to be said that all prophets came to advise mankind and to put them on the right way. Mostly people are running in the wrong direction and finally this will make them repent. Like on the motor way there are no u-turns. You have to wait until you come to an exit. On the motor way you may lose half an hour, but what about your life? You are only given one chance.

SEVEN STEPS

Everything belongs to Him. He is the owner, He is the Creator, we are not. Don't run after *dunya* saying that you are the owner. This *dunya* does not belong to us.

We believe in Holy Books, not in the imagination of philosophers. This world has existed for 7000 years. Once, after the morning prayers, Muhammad* was asking if anyone had a dream. Someone stood up and said, "Last night I dreamt a very peaceful dream which made me so happy. I dreamt that I was in a huge plain, so big that you could not see where it began and where it ended. There was a *mimbar* there with 7 steps. (New reformers in Islam are now producing *mimbars* with 3 steps!) I saw that you, Muhammad*, were stepping up to sit on the 7th step."

"This is a sign that I am the Seal of Prophets. There will be no prophecy and no prophet after me. The 7 steps are a sign that *dunya* has the period of 7000 years for the children of Adam. I was sitting on the 7th step, a sign of the beginning of the 7th period of 1000 years."

"What will come after that?"

"The time which belongs to the End of Time." This is the

time we are in. Everything Muhammad* has informed us of, has happened. One Ramadan has just passed and now we are running to the second one, but we don't know if we will reach it, or in which condition we will be. The numbers of Ramadan are in limits, whether we will have 2000, 1500 or 1600, is arranged according to the Will of Allah. 1500 have passed. We will not have another 100. Every day there are new signs of the End of Time.

Even if you live 1000 years you will face death one day. Everyone must face the Angel of Death. Think about how you will meet him. He will come in two kinds of clothes. One is dressed in mercy, the other as a curse. You don't know which day you will be invited, don't say that you are not ready. Be ready for the Divine Presence, be prepared always!

Don't let your name be written on the list of bad servants. Such people will have never-ending sufferings. *Dunya* is running towards its last station. The second millennium is approaching with many changes. This is a Christian calendar. There are only 2 more years until the year 2000 when unexpected huge events will happen, terrible and horrible wars, because people are following satan and devils and are trying to make even more evil. The result is a Heavenly Punishment. Run to Allah, run to His Shelter! If He shelters you nothing will harm you here or in the hereafter.

NOTHING REALLY EXISTS

Is it possible for an ant to understand a bee? Is it possible for a cat to understand a dog? If a cat isn't a dog, he cannot know the real position of a dog. A dog will understand a dog, a cat will understand a cat. Everyone understands their own level. An ant cannot understand a man. All it knows, is that if it lands under the foot of a man, it will be finished. It knows we are a great creature which moves, but it cannot give any description.

Only a man can know about another man. A man cannot even know about a woman, just like a woman cannot know 100% about a man, because they are fully different beings. So how could it be possible for mankind to understand the Creator? Only another creator could do that. But there cannot be two creators, it is impossible. The greatness of the Creator is that He knows everything, every detail of His creatures.

One divided by infinity is zero. That means nothing is in existence. Every part of your body can be divided to the point of zero. Infinity multiplied by zero is zero. What we are seeing is in reality nothing, shadows. You look into the mirror and you think it is you, but in reality it is just your image, your shadow. Every part which is in existence can come to a point where it cannot be divided anymore.

The Creator in His endless Oceans of Wisdom and His Will creates countless universes, worlds, servants, creatures and kinds of creatures. He calls them, "Come into existence!" and they appear. If He tells them to go, they will disappear in His endless oceans. No-one can refuse His Will. Man must know that they are nothing. When they admit this, they will lose the pride which prevents them to be in the service of the Lord.

People do not even have the most simplest knowledge about the Creator today, even though they do not even have any real existence! That in the mirror is not you! A photograph doesn't exist, even if it looks like it. Everything you see is an image: nothing!

On the Night Journey Allah said to his beloved servant, "I will make you a mirror of me!" This is why we are saying, "*La illaha illa'Llah, Muhammadur Rasul Allah*!"

A television would be nothing without a screen, without it nothing can be seen. If you would change the material of the screen it also would not show. In the same way. Muhammad* is the only one who can serve this purpose. Without his creation nothing could be in existence. In the coming years of the second millennium such real realities of the Lord Almighty Allah will appear.

This is like a feast where the elephant who comes would take its provision, just like the ant would. This is a power station and everyone who comes here will take their share, whether they are aware of it, or not.

THE RIGHTS OF THE LORD

Allah supports those who have good intentions in their hearts. So many people come and complain about their situations and I understand that they are not getting Divine Support. If you get Divine Support everything will be all right. Everyone who complains about their situations must once more have a look at their habits and find out what kind of relationship they are having with their Lord.

When a car stops it is important to see what is wrong with the machine. If you do not find the mistake you will not be able to move. Make a check-up! So many people make check-ups with their physical beings, but they do not bother about their spiritual being, about their relationship with their Lord.

Allah supports true ones, He will never let them down. He supports His trustworthy ones because they are the inheritors of the Prophet* who are always in Divine Service. If anyone wants to improve their situation and save themselves, they must make their Divine Service their priority.

As long as you are giving more value to this worldly life and putting your Divine Service in second place, you are not a true and trustworthy one. It is the most important lesson for mankind.

When you are given honour you are also given responsibility. In an empire the King and Queen deserve the highest respect because they carry the highest responsibility. Those who carry responsibility will be asked, "Did you use your authority to urge my servants to give me the highest respect?" It is not easy to be a king, a queen, a governor or a minister. Allah will ask them first, "Oh my servant, I dressed you in majestic clothes and people were respecting you and bowing to you. If I had not dressed you no-one would listen to you, you would be like others. I chose you. Have you used your power to call people to my Divine Service?"

Someone who is responsible for 10 people or more will come into the Divine Presence on Judgement Day. Allah will ask these 10 people, "My servant was responsible for you. Did he give you your rights and urge you to give your highest respect to me?" If these people say that he did his best, he will be blessed.

If people now would do a referendum in all the countries of the world asking that question, I do not think that people would give their governments a good report. Governments are only concerned about giving their people work, make them earn money and pay income tax. That is the priority of every government. They do not ask what their citizens are doing in respect of the rights of their Lord. They only ask for human rights. What about the rights of the Lord of Heavens?

We need to make a u-turn. The direction we are on is the worst and most dangerous. One day London might be gone. One day Paris may be gone. One day the whole of the Western civilisation might be gone. One day the whole of the Oriental civilisation might be gone. One day everything on earth might be in ruins and people's bodies burnt. Satan and his devils will be the only ones laughing. Allah the Almighty is giving His first chance to governments. They may issue laws for people to obey. Just like cameras catch you speeding and the governments punish you if you do. In the same way governments could prevent evil, but they are not using that power. This is why they will be the first ones to be punished.

We cannot do anything for our children and save them from the hands of devils. If you try, the governments will even tell you off. Children must be free! What foolishness is this? Which religion is saying this? We are under the control of devils and the devils will destroy us. Governments should give their Divine Service first and then the other services. Every department, factory and schools should first give their high respect and then start their work. If not, no blessings will come on earth. This applies from east to west, from north to south.

Everyday when you open the television there are bad news. I don't like to see it. It makes me sad and can occupy my heart for several days. It makes you lose your peace. I never advise people who are worshipping to watch news. It will take away the peace in their hearts.

This is Holy *Ramadan*, a month of peace. But only the ones who are fasting will know this. Those who do not respect and keep the rights of this Holy Month, will never get to know this peace. Those who know this peace should try to extend it until after Ramadan and keep it for their whole life.

People ask for peace through material aspects. Don't think that richness gives you peace, that gold and jewels will bring you peace, that beauty or youth will give you peace. It is temporary. The time of your youth is not permanent. Every day you will lose a bit of it. It cannot give you peace. As long as you are dependent on material aspects you will have a heavy burden which will make you weaker and weaker, like someone loading himself with a heavy stone. Materials make people like a carton, unable to taste this life.

Try to achieve peace through spiritual aspects. The strongest of which you can find in this month. You will feel day and night that you are for Allah. In the daytime you are fasting for Him, in the night you are praying for Him. Feed you spirituality instead of your animal, your ego. Your soul belongs to Heavens, feed it through spiritual ways just this one month. During 11 months you are looking after your physical bodies. Give this one month to Him!

HEALING

Real healing is to be able to send rays of power through your hands to the body of the patient who must be ready to receive the healing. Mostly people are closed and it is impossible even for prophets to reach them. A closed socket cannot transport electricity. On a patient like that you must try to crack open a weak point of their shell from where you can enter.

Since the beginning of time people have been in need of healing, physically and spiritually. Authorised healers will always be on earth. Many of them are totally hidden and you would never imagine them having such powers. If someone is seriously looking for them, they will find. It is not something you can find in books. Not every healer is authorised. Sometimes an unauthorised healer can become infected himself, because he does not have any protection. He can be affected by powerful currents of ill-being from the patient which are transferred to him and make him weak and unable to do anything. He will feel tired because he is only running on a battery, instead of being connected to a stream of power. If he was, he could treat hundreds of patients without being affected.

A healer who comes into such an unprotected situation should quickly take a bath and change his clothes. Also step by step stop drinking alcohol and smoking.

بِسْمِ اللَّهِ الرَّحْمَنِ الرَّحِيمِ

ASKING TO BE CURED

The first thing a patient must do, is to say, "I am Your servant. I have become weaker through this illness. I know it is a result of my bad actions, my sins. Please give me Your Forgiveness for the sake of your most beloved and precious servant." If you ask for the respect of His most respected one, *shifa* will be given to you. According to the level of your belief, it can be given to you instantly, after one hour, one day, 3 days, one week, or after one month. After 40 days it must be taken away from you! Allah will ask you, "What do you want to use your health for?" If you ask for health and strength, you must do it with the intention to serve Him more, not to run even faster after this world. Everything is under His Will, no-one can go against it. It is the base of every building. With a strong foundation you can have a strong belief which will give you pleasure. You will never be sorrowful.

Once Hajaj ordered a companion to be killed. The companion was smiling all along, because he was accepting the Will of His Lord. That is the highest level of belief. You must know that Allah has given us endless levels of belief. A worshipper follows the orders of Allah, but a servant will also follow His Will.

Aziz Mahmud Hudaye was the Sheikh of Sultan Ahmed who built the Blue Mosque in Istanbul. When you enter it you have the feeling that you are entering paradise. The Sultan himself helped putting the stones and soil on the foundation, like a labourer. Every Sultan must have a Sheikh, because if a sultanate is not supported by spiritual power it cannot exist, it must fall.

During his reign a heavy illness befell the people of the time. They fell ill in the morning and were dead by the evening. People were prayed on and buried all day long. A great fear spread over the land. The scholars decided to get together and to go to the Sheikh and ask him to make a prayer asking Allah the Almighty to remove this punishment from his people. The Sheikh opened his door and told them to come in. "Oh our master, you know which terrible illness has befallen us. We are in fear. Please make a *du'a* which Allah will accept to remove this curse."

"I understand that you want this. But until now I have never asked to remove anything which Allah has ordered. I have never asked to change His Will. I am sorry, I cannot do what you are asking for."

The people were sorry and started to cry. But Allah doesn't want His servants to be hopeless, so the Sheikh continued, "Oh you servants, this is my way. But I can send you to someone who can do what you are asking for. I am sending you to a huge cemetery, so frightening that people normally do not even want to go there during the day. Deep in there you will find a *meshtub*, who is occupied with the love and the respect of his Lord. He is on another level all together, attracted to the Divine Level. Beware, it is not easy to come close to him! When he sees you coming, he will attack you with stones and words. Don't give up, tell him that I have sent you!"

It happened the way the Sheikh had told them, and when they mentioned the name of the Sheikh to the *meshtub*, he said, "Oh my brothers, give my respects to him. I will do what he asks of me. I am under his command. Go back to the mosque and pray for the illness to go away, and it will."

The people returned, and as he had said, the illness finished with their prayer.

Allah the Almighty has such servants, when they ask for something, it will happen at once. Keep your respect for everyone, they can be hidden ones. You may lose a big chance to get their prayers and *du'as*.

HEALTHY DIET: DON'T EAT PLASTIC!

Try to eat as much organic food as possible. Eat the red and the white part of meat. Eating only the red will harm the body. Use both of them, it will not make you fat. Your body needs it. If you don't, your body will get weaker and weaker. Such foolish diets turn the flesh into water. So many people have cancer because they have no defence in their body against cancer cells. They also don't drink soup, they only eat fish and chips and fish and chips. This is not good for the body, or kebab, kebab... again the kebab meat does not include the white of the meat. This harms the body and weakens it.

People must try to use the old ways of cooking. Young people can eat more sweets, but the Oriental kinds: Pakistani, or Turkish or Arabic. The European sweets are not good. They do not give the body any nourishment, they are made of plastic. I also don't like to touch chicken nowadays because they are usually artificial, which I have no interest to eat. I like mutton or lamb. I also do not like to eat beef. The flesh of goats gives our skin and our flesh more power. Geese are also still natural and not destroyed by artificial hormones, as well as ducks. That is good for the body. Wild animals are also good to eat.

"Is it all right to eat animals when they have been shot?"

If they have said, "Bismillah!", then it is all right.

Raisins with seeds, nuts and almonds give the body strength.

Change your diet! Nowadays everything is programmed by people who want to control you. They want you to eat as they like. They want you to do as they like. They want you to sleep as they like. You must speak as they like. You must break through their programme and not eat as they like you to. Try to use your own free will and not be lead by them. Use grains, like rice, which have not been affected too much artificially.

Try not to use those foolish drinks. Take away 7up, Coca-Cola and Fanta from your tables, also juices of this and that. Whatever you buy will have something inorganic in it as a preservative which will affect your physical body. I do not like any drink except water to be put in front of me. Even the artificial mineral water. They all harm the body. Drink tap water! People are trying to make a handful of people multimillionaires. They tell us to drink Coca-Cola, Pepsi-Cola, Diet Coke... so many drinks, only to enrich those handful of people. What are the benefits of all those drinks? Do they improve our digestion? In some areas water is not good for drinking, then you can buy bottled water.

Fruit juices I also don't like, because usually they too have preservatives. Make your own! But why? Whenever you make fruit juices there is so much waste which you don't use. Eat the whole fruit! We used to make a lot of different syrups. Sometimes we used the leaves of roses and made rosewater, so delicious.

Cane sugar is the best, or carob or fruits. Be natural!

GENETIC ENGINEERING: DON'T INVOLVE YOURSELF IN THE WILL OF THE CREATOR

The sign of perfection of a servant is to accept everything. A perfect person will see everything which happens in the past, present or future as perfect. If we see anything which is imperfect, it is perfect in its imperfection. The highest *adab* of a servant is to be able to see everything as perfect. Could you imagine a *wezir* in the presence of a sultan to say that something is wrong, even if he was allowed? Never! This is how people should behave towards each other, so how about towards Allah?

Imam Ghazzali said, "It is impossible for anything more suitable for this time to be in existence now. Tomorrow it may be changed." Servants must learn to accept everything from the Lord in an excellent way and to say, "As You like! What You did is perfect." This is the highest level a servant can reach. Any objection would be an involvement in His Will meaning to put your will above His. That is the biggest sin, to want to prevent His Will. If you do, it is possible that something could appear in the beginning which you like, but then something much more powerful will develop which is out of your control.

For example: people wanted to put a barrier in front of the River Nile to cause it to run the way they wanted, not the way the Lord wanted. What is the result of this involvement? Now the River Nile is going deeper than the 100 meter deep columns carrying the foundation of the dam, and the water is starting to creep through it. After some time it will be torn down and all of Egypt will drown. It is a teaching not to involve in such matters.

Today someone wrote me a letter telling me of a rose she had given me a few days ago. She thought it was a normal rose, but then she understood that it only had the appearance of a rose. It had sacrificed its smell to be able to grow quicker. Man had genetically interfered and made the rose grow in a few hours, what would normally take a few days. This is the kind of nonsense involvement mankind is doing now. It will result in a terrible end. Tomatoes are made to grow quickly, in 2-3 hours they get their size. Chicken can reach the size of a 3-4 month old chicken in 3-4 days! All of this harms and destroys people. Terrible involvement from scientists give horrendous harm to the physical body as well as to the spiritual lives of people.

Scientists say that they have to genetically engineer to be able to feed people. They need quick production and quick consumption, because people are wasting in a big way. That which is necessary for mankind is 1% of what they are producing. They throw away 99%. This is why they think they need to interfere. Everything in the life of man is getting worse and worse. People now are brothers of satan because they are wasting. If they wouldn't, the naturally grown food would be enough.

Physically and spiritually people have lost their health. They have no peace, they are punished from both sides. Just this one word of tariqats could save all nations, "Not to involve in the affairs of Allah the Almighty." He knows what is necessary for all nations. They say that the oceans are polluted because so many things are poisoning and killing it. Technology is the greatest danger for everyone. Until it is defeated and thrown away, there will be no more peace physically or spiritually. When Mehdi comes after the biggest war he will be ordered to stop everything by saying, "*Allahu akbar, Allahu akbar, Allahu akbar*!" These three *tekbirs* will destroy technology. It will be finished!

People have been given such a huge power through the use of electricity. But instead of using it for the benefit of mankind, they used it to destroy mankind physically and spiritually. This is why the *tekbir* will destroy the power of electricity and the technology with it.

Try not to be slaves of technology! Avoid it as much as possible and use less and less. Try to use natural ways, if you have a choice. Live your life with nature. Don't run away from nature. If you run away from nature everything which is against nature will follow you, destroy you and kill you! The best is to be as Allah asks you to be: simple! Be free! Don't let anyone force you and employ you as their servant. Make yourself free of technology. Everything Allah has created is excellent and best.

When your thoughts become clean, you will be clean of everything. As long as your mind is dirty you cannot reach cleanliness, which means there is no rest for you physically or spiritually. People are now losing their spiritual balance, so they decline spiritually and physically. Beware and keep good behaviour in front of Allah. Whatever Allah says is right! When He says something is wrong, then it is wrong. If you want to know what is right or wrong use the balance of Islam, the balance of the *Shariah* which is the balance of Heavens. If it is good, keep it. If it is bad, leave it! Try to come from badness to goodness. Don't allow yourself to run from goodness to badness. That is rebellious. The first rebellious one was satan. May Allah help us to change our direction from a bad to a right direction.

بِسْمِ اللَّهِ الرَّحْمَنِ الرَّحِيمِ

HORMONES DESTROYING OUR FOOD

It is so difficult to find clean food to eat. Everything is mixed up with *haram*, with forbidden things. Acceptable worshipping also depends on eating and drinking clean. When we eat *halal* our souls enjoy too and we become healthy. Unclean eating cause headaches and destroys our health. So many illnesses come from wrong eating habits.

Doctors say that they have never before heard of all the new kinds of illnesses. They are all results of bad eating habits. The worst reasons are hormones, they are changing our health. Every kind of meat, vegetable and fruit is filled with hormones, even though it is the most dangerous for mankind. It is *haram* to feed yourself or your children like that.

All the people of the 20th century are asking for is profits. They have a kind of egoistic illness. Everyone is asking to save more and more money. This is the worst characteristic of the ego. Everyone wants to be rich. Everyone wants to be a millionaire, a multimillionaire. Our ego advises us to save money, more and more. It is the advice which satan is giving. People believe that when they have saved billions they will reach happiness and the final target of all their desires. Everything is produced in a way to make lots of money. People have been trained to waste as much as possible so that they can buy new all the time. This is why there is not enough *halal* production available. Everything is done in a gigantic way in huge farms with hormones. There are only about 10 enormous corporations world-wide which are in competition with each other. They hit two birds with one stone: first they produce bad quality food for people and make huge profits. By that people lose their health and then another big firm will produce the medicine for them. How clever!

These eating habits result in the worst illnesses. People are running to the doctors worried about their health. I never find any home without medicine. They even give me vitamin C to make a horse out of me! Everyday I am getting stronger, that is what I believe!

First come the weapons factories, second the medicine and drugs factories, third petroleum, fourth cement... All this is in the hands of the mafia. There are seven or nine big mafia who are famous. No-one is able to stop them.

In this century every badness attacking humanity has spread from east to west, including the Islamic world. We are stepping into a new century. People are weak and without hope concerning their crisis. They do not know what they can do. Their minds have stopped. They may produce treatment to their drugs crisis or terrorism crisis, but without solving it. This is America, the biggest and most powerful station on earth, but they are showing their weakness in front of terrorism. Their most powerful technology cannot be used against it. Allah has caused the mind of man to stop. In which ever direction they run they see that the way is closed. Allah has only left one way open: His Way and His Rules! You must come to His Rules, or you will be finished. It doesn't matter if the whole of mankind will kill each other. They are punishing themselves by themselves.

Democracy, hypocrisy, Stalinism, communism, socialism, capitalism... all is finished. Submit to Heavenly Rules and Heavenly Commands! 24 hours are enough. No need for 2 days, six months or one year, no! If this country would accept Heavenly Rules every economical crisis and terrorism of the whole world would be solved. Oh people, you must help! Allah says that if you help to stop evil, Allah will help you. If you don't care, you will get no Divine Help, no Heavenly Support. Try to help!

SHADOW BEINGS

Allah is the Great. Absolute greatness belongs to Him and absolute real existence belongs to Him. We are shadow beings. We are not real beings, but shadow beings. Not the kind of shadow which you can see when the sun is reflecting. You think that the image you see in the mirror is you, but you cannot touch it or feel it. When you disappear, so does the image. It does give you some understanding about yourself. If you would not see the reflection in the mirror, you would not know at all how you look. Your eyes can see everything except yourself. You can see your body, but your identity is in your face. This is why your identification on a photograph is always your face. You will not be known by your legs, hands or your belly!

You are known by your face. Someone once said, "If I look at the backside of a man's head, I can easily know about his mind, if he is clever or not." So then, what about his face? His face is like a book of his personality. By seeing his face I can understand everything. Nowadays when you buy a new machine you will get an instruction booklet with it. In the same way there are people who look with Divine Lights. Most people just look, they don't see. The ones who are able to see, must be equipped with Heavenly Lights, like Holy People. They look, see and recognise the identity of people, can tell you who you are and for which purpose you have been created. They are real guides, they have x-ray vision.

Your identity is on your face but you cannot see it. You need a mirror to be able to arrange your physical and your spiritual life. For both sides you need a mirror, a guide. Without a mirror you are like a blind person. The mirror will make regular check-ups with you, physically and spiritually. People run to have check-ups on their physical bodies. But they only make very short check-ups on their spiritual beings. A spiritual check-up includes a physical one. It covers everything, like the atmosphere. If you are in it you can see your atmosphere, as well as your world. But if you are only in the world, that is all you will see. This is why the spiritual check-up is the most important one. But people are not interested in such things. They run to their physical check-up which gives them nothing. We need to have a look at ourselves. When you do, you check-up the reality in which you are. You will find out what you need, should you be invited to the Divine Reality. The first mirror of checking-up our spiritual beings are prophets. After that their deputies, the companions. Then all the Holy People, the Saints. If you don't find any of those, you will come and go without knowing about yourself. You may be in the Divine Presence bringing a disliked image of yourself causing others to run away from you, hate you, swearing at you or even attacking and cursing you. The angels will ask you, why you didn't use your long life to have yourself checked. Allah is the real existence. He has no shadow. He is unique.

No Prophet Ever Had Two Faces

Run away from artificial things. Don't be artificial. What I mean by that is: official. When people become official, they lose sincerity. We are not in court here. Those who are artificial are different on the inside from outside. Show yourself as you are. No prophet ever had two faces. No saint does. The Lord of Heavens doesn't like it. Maulana Rumi said, "Be like you show yourself to people!" Sometimes you give a good show to others, but you don't feel like it inside. Try to be the way you are showing yourself. This is an excellent target to try to reach for everyone. Everyone wants to make a good impression on others so that they will not hate him. No-one likes to be hated. Everyone wants to be respected, loved and accepted in the community. This is a deep desire within us. What we show when we are in the community we should try to be.

Especially women want to be attractive. They never want others to be like them. It is an excellent characteristic to want to be unique, but it should be used for a good purpose, not to show off by putting others down. Men too want to be unique. This is a secret characteristic which comes form the Creator to His servants. Everyone has been created in a different form. You cannot find two identical people, not even twins. The Lord is one, He has unity. When He created mankind as His deputies everyone wanted to be in unity, to be unique. No-one wants anyone else to be like themselves. This is why people want to show themselves in the optimal way in the community. It is not right just to do that when others are looking, and then to change when you are alone, it would be a bad characteristic. Be as you show yourself! If you don't, try to!

Everyone must go to the Lord of Heavens. No-one has a permanent residence in this life. We are all temporary. When I come here the immigration officer asks me how long I want to stay. When I say, "2 months!" he will give me 6 months. Even if I would stay for 100 years, it would still be in limits and I would have to go. Those who don't want to go will be taken by Heavenly Beings by force. It is a temporary life.

In the traditional books brought to us by the prophets we learn Heavenly Knowledge. In one of those articles we are being told that when a person dies and is put in a coffin and brought to the cemetery, he will be addressed by the Lord, "Oh my servant...". He will be asked 10 questions. "...you know that during your life you were taking so much care about your appearance... Were you aware of the Lord looking at your heart and that you should try to make your heart look its best?" That is the first question. "Every part of you belongs to you, only your heart is mine."

Especially in our days people are so interested to show themselves in the best way, forgetting that the day will come when they will be going to the Divine Presence of the Lord. Every lady wants to be seen as beautiful. Real beauty is a grant from Heavens to His servant. Someone can be young, but except from having a fresh skin, no good feeling comes from them. Some old ladies have been granted lights on their faces which makes them more beautiful than any young person.

There is a tale from India: there are all kinds of vegetation there that do not grow anywhere else. There is a very strange plant there with the most beautiful scenting flower. Whoever reaches and starts to wear that plant will be loved by everyone because they will feel an unimaginable familiarity to them. Don't think it is easy to find, it grows in the midst of cobras. Because it is so precious, people are prevented form taking it. You cannot reach it without sacrificing. That is an unchanged rule: if you want to reach something precious, you must sacrifice. If you want to reach Paradise, you must sacrifice to enter. People think that it is free, but it isn't. Sacrifice this life to your Lord and He will give you the next. A billion Christians are saying that Jesus was on the cross and sacrificed himself. I am now speaking on their level. He sacrificed his soul and reached to his Lord. The beehive is full of honey. If you are not patient in taking the honey, you cannot reach it. You must pay for everything which is precious. You can find shells on the beach, but they are empty. Pearls are under the sea, and they too are protected by sharks. All Holy People and Prophets are telling us that every night our Lord is looking at His servants to see if anyone is thinking about Him, or if they are all sleeping. We are asking for so many things. In the night when He is looking at us, why aren't we looking at Him? He is telling us to stand up, to come into His Divine Presence and to ask Him what we are asking for. When we ask for something we must sacrifice our sweet sleep, even if it is only for 10 minutes. The longer you stay with Him the more grants He will bestow on you.

Within our traditional knowledge we have been told that if a person gets up in the last part of the night and asks His Lord for this and that, Heavenly enlightened clothes will come on him. A person who is with His Lord by night will be more beautiful during the day, he will be enlightened. You will not have to go to India and to look for the plant. Try to take more and more lights from Heaven. One day you will need them. Particularly when you leave this life and you are accompanied by lights, your soul will not go through darkness, it will go through enlightened worlds. Enlightened people are beloved.

On Judgement Day everyone will have to come to the plain. People will be divided into two parts: enlightened and dark. Look after yourself! If you want try to come enlightened into the Divine Presence. You have a chance now. Don't stay in darkness. If someone is with their ego they will be in darkness. Those who go on the path of the Prophets, will be enlightened. The last target of mankind is to leave this world enlightened.

INTERVIEW:
BAYAT, KISSING OF HANDS, TOUCHING WOMEN, ISLAMIC CLOTHES...

Q: Many oppose to people taking bayat with you. If we have given our bayat to the Prophet*, why do we have to give it to you too?

S.N: Who are we giving our bayat to? Like the *Sahaba* we have Muhammad* in front of us. We have been ordered to give our oath to true people, to a Sheikh.

Q: Is it a necessity in Islam to give your bayat to a Sheikh, like the sahabas after the passing away of Muhammad* gave their bayat to Abu Bakr Siddiq?

S.N: Yes! Until 1924 every Muslim would give their oath to the Sultan, who was representing the Prophet*.

Q: Is this like when the Prophet* told us that when there are 3 or more of us we should elect an emir?

S.N: No, an emir is something else. Not everyone we call an emir is an emir. A real emir must have power. Emir means a sultan, a shadow of Heavens on earth. You must give your oath to him. You must obey, that is what *bayat* means.

Q: Who are the inheritors of the Prophet? The people with Islamic knowledge?*

S.N: That is not enough. It has to do with spirituality.

Q: Do the followers of the Sheikh have to follow him blindly?

S.N: Never blindly! The Prophet* had open eyes and his followers must too!

Q: Many people think that having bayat with a Sheikh is like following a dictator.

S.N: When you take a plane, you also put your trust into the pilot. You wouldn't think of telling him how to do it. The same with doctors, people do whatever the doctors tell them to. If you had eyes that could see everything, you wouldn't need a Sheikh. We want to open the eyes of our people, not make them blind.

Q: People object on your hands being kissed.

S.N: I am not a sultan. Let people go and kiss their hands! These people are envious, because they are not giving full respect to their Lord. If they were, people would respect them. Maybe I am respected in the Divine Presence and that is why people run up to me. I am not begging people to come up to me and to kiss my hands! They rush on me from all over the world and I do not tell them to go away. Why should I? Are my hands dirty? If they were I would prevent it. But the hands of the people who oppose this are dirty with their dirty works. When people come close to a blessed person they feel familiarity and want to kiss and embrace. When a person wants to show their respect by kissing the hand it is not prohibited in the Islamic *Shariah*. No-one can bring any evidence that Muhammad* did not allow it.

Q: But not only men are kissing your hand, but women too. Is that allowed in Islam?

S.N: Do they have evidence on that? If that was prohibited we would not be allowed to approach our women. They have no *fiqh*.(Quran, *Surat* 4, *Ayat* 43 and *Surat* 5, *Ayat* 6).You may touch.

Q: For the mahram, or...?

S.N: ...*an Nissa*, is *alif lam* a sign for all women, or just for some? There is a secret reality there: you can touch a lady, but if your ego awakes with a bad desire it is prohibited. A person may touch his daughter or his mother and it is not prohibited. He may touch his wife and it could be prohibited. Nothing awakes in a person with his *mahram*. But if it is not a *mahram* it is dangerous. That is why the *Shariah* prevents you to touch without a reason. Otherwise a doctor couldn't touch the body of a woman. No-one objects to the millions of ladies who every day go to the doctor and show everything. It did not exist at the time of the Prophet*. When they give birth they show themselves completely! How can that be? Why do people not complain about that? Instead they come to me, a person who is 80 years old! The *Shariah* does give the permission for the hands of prophets and their inheritors to be kissed. I do not tell the ladies to come and kiss my hand. No! They come to give their respects. I cannot refuse it, because I am calling Europeans, non Muslims, into Islam. They are still new and if I would prevent them from kissing my hand their hearts would be broken. They would accuse Islam of having no gentleness. We are not living in Saudi Arabia, Libya, Algeria, Turkey, Iran or in Pakistan! I am calling people here, in Europe. This is why we can use the methods which the Prophet* was using at the beginning of Islam. People at that time were also not using scarves. For the first 13 years in Mecca, they were mixing freely with men and not wearing scarves. All that came in Medina. The people who are accusing me of these points have no understanding of Islam. They are scholars, but empty!

Q: According to the Hanafi school what are the rules of a woman touching you without desires? Would you need an ablution?

S.N: All the four schools of thought were going to agree on this point, but then *Imam Shafi* prevented it. He wanted to close the door of *fitna* which arises by young people touching each other. *Abu Hanifa* gave the permission under a condition: if your feelings do not change and become *haram*, it is all right. If they do, it is prohibited in the school of *Abu Hanifa* too. When feelings change, our body awakens and we discharge, making our *wudu* invalid.

Q: Why are people so attracted to you?

S.N: They are spiritually attracted because their souls are swimming in the same pool as my soul: in the ocean of mercy. Their souls are familiar to me. I have been with them since the Day of Promises, whether they are aware of it, or not. I am reaching to every sultan on earth now, because their time is approaching. All presidents will come down. In the 21st century presidents, democracy and parliaments will go. The sultans will come. This has been written in all the Holy Books: the Old Testament, the New Testament and the Holy Quran.

Q: Many people say that Islam does not have to be demonstrated in your clothes, that it is better to have it in your heart.

S.N: These people are fully foolish! They are making propaganda for the satanic school. Why do armies keep their uniform? If clothes were not important, tell the generals to start wearing civil clothing instead or the Pope or the Patriarch. Do you think it has no meaning? Why are only Muslims getting these silly questions?

Q: People say that if the Prophet* would come today, he would be wearing the clothes of today; jeans and a suit.

S.N: Jeans are very unhealthy clothes. The traditional Muslim clothes are very healthy. But people do not understand such things. They want to follow fashion, and they want to prepare all other Muslims to do the same, to follow their ugly fashions! We do not need to follow any body's fashion. We have our own originality and our own tradition in our way of dressing and in everything else too. Only weak people need to follow powerful people. We are honoured to have our own way of dressing. If people have a job where it is necessary to wear another style, that is all right.

At the time of the Sultan someone came and asked the Grand Mufti: "I just bought a cow, and every time I come to milk it, it refuses, because it was accustomed to the old owner who was always wearing a hat. Would you permit me to wear a hat during the time I milking?"
"Yes, as long as you are milking, it is all right!" So this applies to all Muslims living in non Muslim countries.

Q: Harvard University is making a research into the suggestion that the 21st century will be a century of spiritualism.

S.N: Harvard University is a serious university. They are looking into a very important point. But how are they doing it? The target is like an island in the ocean. In front of them are Christianity, Judaism and Islam. All of them have vessels, but the vessel of Christianity is 2000 years old, the vessel of Judaism 4000 years old, the Islamic one is the newest one. If you had to choose for a long and dangerous travelling, would you use the oldest or the newest vessel? That is the question I would like to raise to the people of Harvard! They must accept the newest vessel which is most intact, powerful and strongest, not the rusty old ones.

UNIFYING HEARTS

Why did the companions of the Prophet* gather around him? They were not forced, they were not paid, they were loved! People run to love. They hate bad characteristics and bad things. They like love, and that is what the companions of the Prophet* were passing on. Allah filled the heart of Muhammad* with love and that is what he gave to his followers. Without love there is no taste within faith. In every religion love is the first power. When your heart has opened up to love for the Prophet* you will accept that he is a messenger. When you love you will respect and you will follow. You cannot follow anyone without love.

ANGELS OF PROTECTION

There is no protection, except from Allah. Sayyidina Ali* appeared one night to a group of his followers in their tent. It was on a battlefield and he had crossed the enemy's side without any bodyguards. They asked him in surprise why he was doing something as risky as that. "Don't you believe that Allah the Almighty puts *Angels of Hafasa* to protect you? He puts one in the front and one behind. If it is the will of Allah the Almighty for something to come on a servant, the angels will not prevent it. If Allah has not given permission for anything harmful to reach a servant, the angels will cover you from front to back. Don't worry, you are companions!"

PROPHECY: THE FIRST UNIVERSITY

Mankind is divided into two kinds of people. One of them have their total interest in this world. They are like sheep, busy with what they are eating and drinking, only interested in their stomach, their physical body and how to deal with their physical desires.

Is there anyone here in the university who is studying for the love of knowledge? Or for the love of wisdom? No! Everyone wants to reach a level of this life, usually the top point. Everyone wants to be number one in this life, to be able to enjoy themselves much more than others. It has been my test for the last 80 years to have to watch people going in that direction. They only want to find ways in which to enjoy themselves even more and fulfil their physical desires more and more. There is only a handful, a minority, who are looking up. I don't think that they are teaching about the history of prophets in the universities. There is no university which is interested in Heavenly Knowledge. They might be teaching philosophy, but not the philosophy of religions, the philosophy of prophets, the philosophy of Heavens. No! If the universities were teaching about prophets and about their historical events, they would find a different perspective than the one we are in.

Prophecy is the first institution on earth, the first school for teaching people. All prophets came to teach people. Mankind is created without any knowledge, but they need knowledge. The Creator wants to teach them about themselves and about Himself. Prophecy was the first university. Prophets came to teach people. What did they teach? Do you think that they came to teach badness and evil and make people suffer? Do you think that the Creator wanted His creatures to suffer? That is impossible! You, as a father, would you want your children to suffer? No! No-one wants their children to suffer. Everyone wants their children to be happy, successful and honoured in their life. You come to learn from your teachers how to be successful, happy and enjoyful in this life.

It is impossible for the Creator, Who created man, to let His creatures suffer. This is why He sent prophets and messengers with His Divine Messages to this world. All prophets came with messages for the salvation of mankind, for their happiness, honour, success and to prevent them from suffering. This much we know, and our minds agree on this point.

COLLECTING HEARTS FOR THE OCEANS OF UNITY

We are asking Allah the Almighty to send us His powerful servants to collect our hearts, not our bodies. Our bodies can be collected by anyone. Someone just has to come with a drum and hundreds and thousands will run after him. That is not a good thing. We are asking for collectors of hearts who will lead you to Allah. When we come to Allah with one heart we will be protected here and in the hereafter. Don't leave the unity! Don't be alone! Be with a group which is in unity for Allah and for His Prophet, may peace be upon him.

We meet in the same ocean, in the ocean of unity of Allah. We ask to enter it, to swim in it forever. We are like drops coming from the clouds, falling into the ocean and becoming the ocean. That is *fana-ul-b'ilLah, fana-ul-fi-Rasul, fana-ul-fil-Sheikh*. Melt your existence and give it. Finish it and Allah the Almighty will dress you in *Wujud-ul-Haqqani*, the appearance of Truth. When you have given this temporary being to Allah, He will grant you from His Divine Existence and will dress you in a body which is real and will be with you forever. You will enter the ocean of unity. There is the ocean of *ahadiya*, of oneness. That is impossible, it is unknown: '*Hu, Hu, Hu, Hu...*' finishing... Then: 'Allah, Allah, Allah...' from *Hu* that is *ghaib-ul-mutlaq*, the absolute secret existence of Allah the Almighty. When He wants His servant to know something He will throw His Holy Name Allah. Prophet

Sayyidina Muhammad* represents this Holy Name. We are trying to bring the hearts of people on that way. Our supporter is Allah, His Prophet* and all his Holy People.

THE EARTH IS YOUR MOTHER

Everything which has a beginning has an ending. You are asking me to stay. But if I was here for 20 years instead of for 20 days and it would end today, it would be the same. In this life this is how it has to be. No-one is together forever, even children and families, neighbours, friends, relatives, *murids* and sheikhs, students and teachers, all go different ways one day.

We can continue in our hearts. We are always together in our souls, even if it is not physical. It tells us that we are servants of Allah the Almighty. All of us are creatures. Even if our clothes change, our original position never will. We are not giving a lecture, I am not a professor but a simple person, like all prophets were. They were sitting on the ground with poor people, slaves, women, children...

We have been created from earth and we must try to be closer to earth. This will give you a good character and make you more humble. If you sit on strange chairs, you think you are important. Being close to earth gives benefit to your body. Scientists tell us that there are so many bacteria there. The closer you come to earth the friendlier they will be with you. They will run after those who escape from them. Just like with dogs: if you are friendly with them, they will be too.

People nowadays are living in skyscrapers far away from earth. They are in concrete buildings surrounded by plastic and metal. They are escaping from nature and all kinds of illnesses come to them. They want to know where cancer comes from. It is because people are running away from nature. Befriend the earth! You have been created from earth and you will return to earth. If not today, then tomorrow, after one week, one month, one year, or even after 100 years. You cannot escape, you will return to earth. Don't run away from earth, it is your mother. If you come closer to earth it will change your nature for the better. It will give your face more lights and take away the darkness. Disturbing bacteria will leave you and you will be more in peace and in comfort.

This is why all prophets used to sit on earth. But nowadays people want to be elegant. Physically you take benefit by sitting close to earth, spiritually even more so. Your spirituality will increase, because you will accept to be humble. No-one can develop spiritually without becoming humble. The most humble person is the highest one spiritually. The characteristic which prevents spirituality is pride. Satan was on the highest position when he was humble, but when he became proud he fell to the lowest. The best quality for a servant is to be humble.

Whoever wants to reach the high stations of Heavens must accept that they are nothing. If you want safety, you must throw your weight away. In the old days when ships were travelling through difficult straits, people would throw their luggage overboard. If you want to reach Heavenly Stations you must throw your burdens overboard. The heaviest part of you is your ego, asking to be something, never sacrificing itself. Sacrifice it! When you have done that, you will reach Heavens and be like lights without any physical body stopping you. It can carry you from earth to Heavens.

SWORD OF PROTECTION

I ask of Allah the Almighty to give me shelter from evil and devils. Only He can shelter us. If He protects, you will be protected. No-one can protect themselves from devils and evil, you must ask Him to protect you. You must know what you are doing and you must do what you understand. Allah the Almighty has given you a sword of protection: *Bismillahi rahmani rahim*. With that you call to Allah and He will grant you a sword with which you can defend yourself.

YOUR CONSCIENCE COMES FROM HEAVENS

As you do not use your conscience, you fall into endless sufferings. This is why I implore you to even for a moment to be with your conscience every night. Make a check-up and ask, "Tell me honestly, was I with *Haqq*, with Truth, today, or not?" Take your answer from your conscience! It will be pure. Your conscience comes from Heavens. It cannot cheat you. It cannot tell lies. It will tell you the truth.

GLOSSARY:

adab: good manners, well behaved

ahadiya: unity

Akhirat: the Hereafter

Al hamdulillah: thanks be to Allah

alif lam: two letters of the Arabic alphabet with which some chapters of the Holy Quran begins. They symbolise hidden meanings only known to people with deep spiritual knowledge.

'Allahu akbar, Allahu akbar, Allahu akbar!': 'Allah is greater, Allah is greater, Allah is greater!'. The beginning of the call to prayer.

an Nissa: Women, the third chapter of the Holy Quran

Angels of Hafasa: the Guardian Angels

Ayat: a verse of a chapter in the Holy Quran

barakat: blessing

bayat: allegiance, to promise to obey

Bismillahi rahmani rahim: in the name of Allah, most merciful, most compassionate. The sentence with which a believer should start every action to ensure that it is blessed

dergha: a meeting place for sufis, renowned for their hospitality

du'a: prayer of supplication

dunya: this worldly life

fana-ul-b'ilLah: to extinguish and become one with Allah

fana-ul-fi-Rasul: to extinguish and become one with the Prophet*

fana-ul-fil-Sheikh: to extinguish and become one with the Sheikh

fiqh: Islamic jurisprudence

fitna: discord

ghaib-ul-mutlaq: unseen infinity

hadith: a description of the detailed behaviour of the Prophet* in everyday situations. These are taken as guidelines for good manners. A *hadith* is only considered to be legally valid if a precise chain of transmission has been recorded.

halwa: an oriental sweet

Hanafi: one of the four schools of thought within the Islamic jurisprudence

haqq: truth, reality. One of the 99 Names of Allah

haqqanis: truthful ones

haram: forbidden. The opposite of *halal*

'Hu, Hu, Hu': 'He, He, He' part of an invocation of Him, the Almighty

Imam Shafi: the founder of one of the four schools of thought within the Islamic Jurisprudence

insha'Allah: so Allah wills

jinn: beings made of smokeless fire who inhabit the earth with us. They are like humans: they can be good or evil and have responsibility because they have been given will-power. They too will be present on Judgement Day. The Quran addresses them too. They are made of different materials than we are, but we live on the same planet, so it is important to know how not to annoy them unnecessarily. Their influence can be noticed in the energy surrounding us. If we are not in unity with the Creator and do not comply to His Rules, they will enforce the feeling of fear. If we are in unity, the presence of the *jinn* can only enforce this reality and we will be even more in unity. Some people are more on the level of *jinn* and more likely to get into contact with them. For them it is very vital to follow every means of protection: to say *bismillah* before any action, to have *wudu* at all times and to be careful not to cut nails or hair after sunset. When you cut them, always either burn or bury them in soil, a flower pot will do. Otherwise you invite the *jinn* to put spells on you. Avoid housework connected to water after sunset, as this is the time most *jinn* are awake. Water has the same reaction on their fire-bodies as fire on ours.

La haula wa la quata ila bila ilathi athim: There is no power and no strength except through Allah, Most High, Most Great

'La illaha illaLah, Muhammadur Rasul Allah': 'No, there is no God except Allah and Muhammad is Allah's Messenger' . The testimony of faith.

La illaha illaLlah: No, there is no God but Allah

Last Days: the days mentioned in all Holy Books as the End of the World

mahram: the 'prohibited' degrees of relationship, i.e., those near blood relatives of the opposite sex with whom marriage is prohibited

Maqqam-ul-Khilafa: the station of the Caliph, of the representative of Allah on earth

Mehdi: the rightly-guided one. The one who at the end of time will lead people to the good side and prepare for the coming of Jesus*. Before his coming there will be Armageddon, the last great war. It will last for 3 months after which *Mehdi* will come. But with him the Anti-Christ, the manifestation of evil, will also appear. For 40 days the 2 of them will roam the earth and everyone will have to choose sides. As the Anti-Christ will use all means to cheat people, he will appear as charming and perform many 'miracles' like waking up the dead, but in fact it is the darkest black magic. Because of this most people, about 6/7 of the world population, will follow him and not recognise the real one, *Mehdi*.

When this division has been completed, Jesus* will return. He will first come down from Heavens to Damascus, to the tomb of John the Baptist*. He will then go to Istanbul and get the flag of Muhammad*, which is kept there at the Topkapi Museum. With this he will rush to Megiddo, the plains south of Nazareth, today Israel. Here he will kill the Anti-Christ. When the Anti-Christ dies, all his followers will go with him and the 40-year-long rule of complete peace on earth, with Jesus* as the King, will begin. Insha' Allah...

meshtub: someone distached from the world out of love for Allah

mimbar: the culpit in a mosque

murids: followers of a Sheikh

Naqshbandiyya Tariqat: tariqat' is the path in Arabic. Sufis, the mystics in Islam, use these 'ways to Heaven' by being taught mystical practices by their sheiks. Originally there were 42 *tariqats*, but the *hadith* has foretold, that at the end of time, these will all dissolve but one, which will unite all *tariqats* under *Mehdi*. It is essential that all these *tariqats* have a continuous line of succession leading back to Muhammad*. In the case of the *Naqshbandia Tariqat*, Sheik Nazim is the 40th Sheik in this chain (see: the Golden Chain of the Naqshbandia Tariqat). We believe him to be the last one in this line of succession before *Mehdi*.

people of The Book: Jews, Christians and Muslims. People who follow at least one of the Holy Revelations: the Old Testament, the New Testament and the Holy Quran (which Sheikh Nazim refers to as the Last Testament)

Qadiri: a Sufi tariqat

Rajab: the 7th month in the Islamic lunar calendar, one of the Holy Months. A month which is dedicated to Allah the Almighty and therefore He should be praised as much as possible. The special *zikr* for this month is 2500 *'La illaha illaLlah'* per day. It is also *sunna* to fast on Mondays and Thursdays. On the 27th of *Rajab* is the ascension of Muhammad*, the Night Journey, on which he was lead by the Archangel Gabriel through the Seven Hells and Seven Heavens to the Divine Presence. Here he was shown exactly how to perform the prayer. We have been created to worship Him, to praise Him, to join with Him.

Ramadan: the 9th month in the lunar calendar, the month of fasting. Muslims are obliged to fast and refrain from any evil intentions from dawn to sunset. It is the month in which the first part of the Holy Quran was revealed to Muhammad* by the Archangel Gabriel.

Sahaba: the companions of the Prophet*

Shariah: the Sacred Law of Islamic jurisprudence. It is based on the Quran and the *hadith*, and is the guideline for every Muslim's conduct, individually and collectively. There are four schools of thought: the Hanafi, Hanbali, Maliki and Shafi'i, which vary only slightly in their interpretation. The Islamic legal system can be summarised as follows: everything is allowed, except that which Allah has prohibited. No human being has the right to change this. The authority to say what is allowed and what is prohibited belongs to Allah alone.

shifa: healing

Surat: a chapter of the Holy Quran

tariqat: see: *Naqshbandiyya Tariqat*

tekbir: the call to prayer

tekke: a meeting place for sufis, renowned for their hospitality

Thora: the Old Testament

ulemas: learned scholars

umma: the community of all Muslims

Wahabis: A political movement of Muslims in Saudi Arabia. They are against any spiritual powers connected to Islam, which is why they do not believe in Holy People or in any form of Holy Energy. They are trying to turn Islam into something intellectual, failing to recognise that it is the spiritual power which opens up people's hearts and makes them willing to submit themselves to the Rules of Allah rather than following their own.

wasila: intermediary

wezir: a minister to the Calipha

wudu: ritual washing of hands, mouth, nostrils, face, forearms, head, ears and feet with running water, to be pure for prayers.

Wujud-ul-Haqqani: the face of Truth, of Reality

zawiya: a meeting place for sufis, renowned for their hospitality

zikr: remembrance and invocation of Allah, typical for Sufis, who by repeating the various Names of Allah, aim to get closer and closer to His Presence.

THE GOLDEN CHAIN OF THE NAQSHBANDIYYA TARIQAT

1. Sayyidina Muhammad,salla-lahu'alayhi wa salam
2. Abu Bakr Siddiq Khalifatu-r Rasouli-Llah
3. Salman Al Farsi
4. Qasim bin Muhammad bin Abu Bakr As Siddiq
5. Imam Abu Muhammad Ja'far As Sadiq
6. Sultan-l'Arifin Abu Yazid Al Bistami
7. Abu-l Hasan Al Kharaqani
8. Abu'Ali Ahmad bin Muhammad Al Farmadi Ar Rudhabari
9. Khwaja Abu Yaqoub Yusuf Al Hamadani
10. Abu-l'Abbas, Sayyidina Khidr'alayhi-s salam
11. Khwaja'Ala'u-d Dawlah'Abdu-l Khaliq Ghujdawani
12. Khwaja'Arif Ar Riwgarawi
13. Khwaja Mahmoud Al Faghnawi
14. Khwaja Azizan'Ali Ar Ramitani
15. Khwaja Muhammad Baba As Sammasi
16. Khwaja Sayyid Amir Al Kulali
17. Imamu-t Tariqati Baha'-d Din An Naqshibandi
18. Khwaja'Ala'u-d din Attar Al Bukhari
19. Khwaja Ya'qoub Al Charkhi
20. Hadrat Ishan Khwaja-i Ahrar'Ubaydu-llah
21. Muhammad Az Zahid Al Bukhari
22. Darwish Muhammad
23. Maulana Ahmad Khwaja Kil Amkanaki As Samarkandi
24. Muhammad Al Baqi'bi-Llah Berang As Simaqi
25. Ahmad Al Farouqi Sirhindi Mujadddidu-l Alfi-th Thani
26. Muhammad Ma'soum bin Ahmad Al Farouqi Sirhindi
27. Sayfu-d din'Arif
28. Sayyid Nour Muhammad Al Bada'uni
29. Shamsu-d din Habibu-Llah Jan-i Janan
30. Abdu-Llah Ad Dihlawi
31. Shaykh Khalid Diya'ud din Al Baghdadi
32. Shaykh Isma'il
33. Khas Muhammad
34. Shaykh Muhammad Efendi Yaraqhi
35. Sayyid Jamalu-d din Al Ghumuqi Al Husayni
36. Abu Ahmad As Sughuri
37. Abu Muhammad Al Madani
38. Sayyid Sharafu-d din Daghistani
39. Sultanu-l Aulia'Maulana'Abdu-Llah Al Fa'izi Ad Daghistani
40. Maulana Muhammad Nazim Al Haqqani An Naqshbandiyya